Writer: Alison Pollet
Editor: Max Greenhut
Editorial Consultant: Michele Millard
Video Researcher: Tera Kuntz
Editorial Director, MTV Books: Eduardo A. Braniff
Director of Development, Bunim/Murray Productions: Scott Freeman

Cover and interior design by EPHEMERA

SPECIAL THANKS TO:
Anne, Dan, Jon, Tara, Noah, Roni, Rachel, Sean, Jon, Cynthia, Eric, Piggy, Christina, Shayne, Kefla, Chadwick and Susie

Scott Bagley, Alicia Bean, Cindy Bradeen, Eduardo A. Braniff, Mary-Ellis Bunim, Robert Caplain, Avery Coburn, David Forrer, Scott Freeman, Irene Fu, Janine Gallant, Richard Glatzer, Melanie Graham, Lauralee Jarvis, Jeff Jenkins, Julie Johns, Patrick Kendall, Mark Kirschner, Andrea LaBate, Michelle Mausser, Laura Murphy, Jonathan Murray, Clay Newbill, Shawn O'Gallagher, Sally O'Neill, Kim Noone, Benjamin Salter, Charlotte Sheedy, Robin Silverman, Donald Silvey

David Ball, Emily Bestler, Gina Centrello, Karen Clark, Twisne Fan, Lisa Feuer, Max Greenhut, Steve Huang, Donna O'Neill, Liate Stehlik, and Kara Welsh

GRATEFUL ACKNOWLEDGMENT MADE TO THE FOLLOWING FOR PROVIDING PHOTOS, JOURNALS, PERSONAL MEMORABILIA, AND SOURCE MATERIAL:
Anne, Dan, Jon, Tara, Noah, Roni, Rachel, Sean, Jon, Cynthia, Eric, Piggy, Christina, Shayne, Kefla, Chadwick and Susie; Weekly World News, p.130

Mary-Ellis Bunim, Cartesia (maps), NBC Photo/Gary Nul, (p.5), Toni Gallagher, The Lake Placid News (article and accompanying photo reprinted with permission, p.65), Steve Longo, Cheryl Martin (picture of Roni, p.14), Michelle Millard, Jonathan Murray, and Clay Newbill

An Original Publication of MTV Books/Pocket Books

POCKET BOOKS, a division of Simon and Schuster, Inc.
1230 Avenue of the Americas, New York NY 10020

Copyright © 1998 by MTV Networks. All rights reserved. MTV Music Television, Road Rules, and all related titles, logos, and characters are trademarks of MTV Networks, a division of Viacom International Inc.

All rights reserved, including the right to reproduce this book or portions thereof in any form whatsoever. For information address Pocket Books, 1230 Avenue of the Americas, New York NY 10020

First MTV Books/Pocket Books trade paperback printing October 1998

ISBN: 0-671-02595-3

10 9 8 7 6 5 4 3 2 1

Printed in the U.S.A.

Pocket and colophon are registered trademarks of Simon and Schuster Inc.

ALISON POLLET

Designed by **EPHEMERA**

BASED ON MTV'S <u>ROAD RULES</u>
CREATED BY MARY-ELLIS BUNIM AND JONATHAN MURRAY
IN ASSOCIATION WITH MTV

MTV Books

Pocket Books

NEW YORK • LONDON • TORONTO • SYNDNEY • TOKYO • SINGAPORE

FOREWORD

HEY, READERS!

This is Anne and Jon from Road Rules Northern Trail and Susie and Kefla from Road Rules Down Under. Nice to meet you and welcome to Road Rules Journals! This book is packed with stuff: interviews, casting applications, pictures, pages from our secret diaries, and all sorts of nifty information you never needed to know—just joking.

Being on Road Rules is a complete trip, no pun intended. It changes your life forever. Living in close quarters with people you've just met, being physically challenged on a daily basis, and traveling across unknown lands while under the constant surveillance of cameras—it can get a little crazy! We know people on TV always say this, but we may be the only ones who can say it and actually mean it: It's not as glamorous as it looks. Seriously! It can get really intense at times—not to mention really exhausting, really dirty, and occasionally smelly!

People are always asking us what being on Road Rules is really like. Well, this book will show you. We're actually letting you see entries from our personal diaries. We're sorry if the handwriting is sometimes hard to read, but be kind and cut us some slack! You try writing in a moving Winnebago while certain automotively challenged cast members are at the wheel! (Don't worry, Roni and Piggy, we're not naming names!)

We hope you dig this book. Remember, even though we say awful, horrible, not-so-very-nice things about each other, we do love one another very much. Really we do. Honestly. It's true. No lies.

X X X O O O,

Kefla   *Susie*   *Jon*   *Anne*

P.S. Check out the Road Rules All Stars section to see how the old pros can stir it up! We're not worthy! We're not worthy!

d Rules trip, our cast members are on camera most of their waking hours (and
ile they're sleeping!). Our crews rotate in and out, communicating to each other
ips are building and what stories they should be "tracking." But despite our best
y interesting moment of the trip, we occasionally miss one or two. That's why
we've given the cast members diaries. If something didn't get caught on cam-
ured by one of the cast members in his or her diary.
d by the directors once a week. In those interviews, they express their feelings
m they're traveling and the experiences they're having. But often, their most
elings are saved for the pages they write in their diaries each day. We have to
ring their words with us. Just think about it: how many of you would show
takes a lot of courage and confidence in yourself to open up to complete
cast members share is visceral, reacting to what's happening at the
ersonal, and they don't hold back! If you find yourself struggling to read
these diaries were written under extreme circumstances—in the dark, in
the Winnebago. And, unfortunately, not all our heroes are good spellers!
u enjoy the section on the Road Rules-All Stars. Viewers loved catching
el, and Sean so much, we went back and did it again—this time with a
keep a look out for the upcoming Road Rules/Real World All Star
te-November 1998, starring Noah, Anne, Roni, Kefla, Kalle, and Mark,
Montana, and Janet. Their escapades take them all over the state of
VE end!

at the Road Rules Journals. It's a rare opportunity to get to know

N MURRAY and MARY-ELLIS BUNIM

THEME SONG

We are brave, we are bold we do nothing we are told
We are prisoners of ROAD RULES show
We are stupid we are lazy! we drive our directors crazy!
We are prisoners of ROAD RULES show
How bravely we stand with matches in our hand
watching the winnie go down in flames

We are brave we are bold We do nothing we are told
We are prisoners of ROAD RULES show!

COMPOSED BY ROAD RULES CAST

NOAH
Birthdate: 6-29-78
Hometown:
Mequon, Wisconsin
Sign: CANCER
Fave Road Snack:
Ritz crackers
Fave Road Tune:
Mick Jagger's
"Don't Tear Me Up"

JON
Birthdate: 12-14-76
Hometown:
Boxboro, Massachusetts
Sign: SAGITTARIUS
Fave Road Snack: Lettuce
Fave Road Tune:
Divine Comedy's "Casanova"

DAN
Birthdate: 2-13-77
Hometown:
Apple Valley, Minnesota
Sign: AQUARIUS
Fave Road Snack:
Beef jerky
Fave Road Tune:
Anything on the
Rolling Stones'
Rewind

TARA
Birthdate: 11-17-77
Hometown:
Chatsworth, California
Sign: SCORPIO
Fave Road Snack:
The salt packets
from Top Ramen packages
Fave Road Tune:
Edie Brickell's "Nothing"

ANNE
Birthdate: 10-30-73
Hometown: Tucson, Arizona
Sign: SCORPIO
Fave Road Snack:
Power Bars
Fave Road Tune:
Dee-Lite's
"Groove Is in the Heart"

RONI
Birthdate: 11-22-78
Hometown:
New York, New York
Sign: SAGITTARIUS
Fave Road Snack:
Baby carrots
Fave Road Tune:
Puff Daddy's
"I'll Be Missing You"

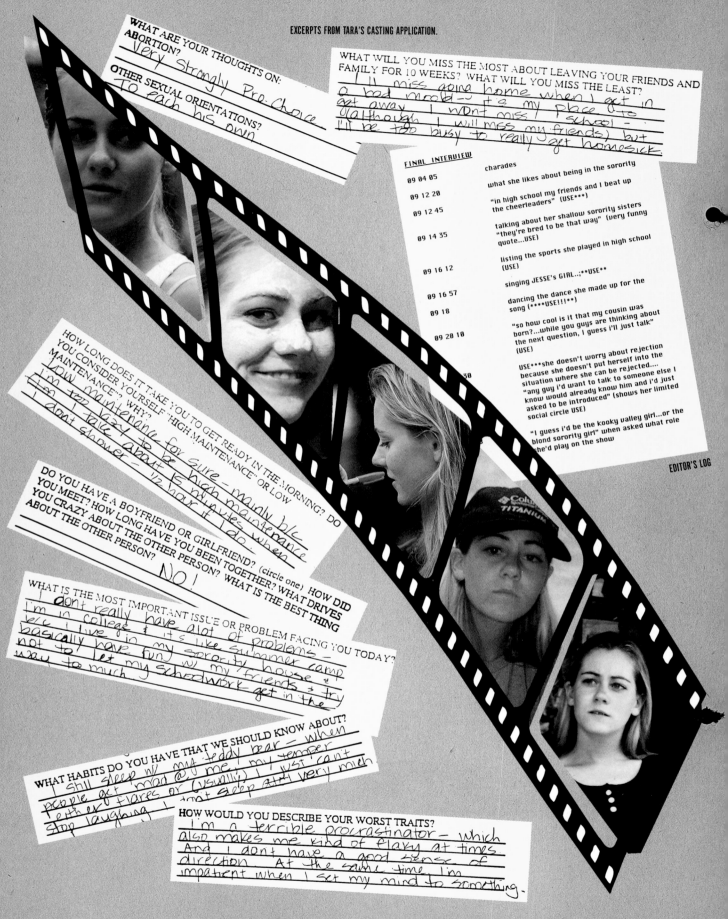

EXCERPTS FROM TARA'S CASTING APPLICATION.

WHAT ARE YOUR THOUGHTS ON:
ABORTION?
Very strongly Pre-Choice

OTHER SEXUAL ORIENTATIONS?
To each his own

WHAT WILL YOU MISS THE MOST ABOUT LEAVING YOUR FRIENDS AND FAMILY FOR 10 WEEKS? WHAT WILL YOU MISS THE LEAST?
I'll miss going home when I get in a bad mood — its my place to get away. I won't miss school — (although I will miss my friends) but I'll be too busy to really get homesick.

FINAL INTERVIEW

	charades
09 04 05	what she likes about being in the sorority
09 12 20	"in high school my friends and I beat up the cheerleaders" (USE***)
09 12 45	
09 14 35	talking about her shallow sorority sisters "they're bred to be that way" (very funny quote...USE)
09 16 12	listing the sports she played in high school (USE)
09 16 57	singing JESSE's GIRL...;**USE**
09 18	dancing the dance she made up for the song (****USE!!!**)
09 20 10	"so how cool is it that my cousin was born?...while you guys are thinking about the next question, I guess I'll just talk" (USE)
30	USE***she doesn't worry about rejection because she doesn't put herself into the situation where she can be rejected.... "any guy I'd want to talk to someone else I know would already know him and I'd just asked to be introduced" (shows her limited social circle USE)
	"I guess I'd be the kooky valley girl...or the blond sorority girl" when asked what role she'd play on the show

EDITOR'S LOG

HOW LONG DOES IT TAKE YOU TO GET READY IN THE MORNING? DO YOU CONSIDER YOURSELF "HIGH MAINTENANCE" OR LOW MAINTENANCE"? WHY?
Low maintenance for sure — mainly b/c I'm too lazy to be high maintenance I don't take about 15 minutes when I take a shower — 1/2 hour if I do.

DO YOU HAVE A BOYFRIEND OR GIRLFRIEND? (circle one) HOW DID YOU MEET? HOW LONG HAVE YOU BEEN TOGETHER? WHAT DRIVES YOU CRAZY ABOUT THE OTHER PERSON? WHAT IS THE BEST THING ABOUT THE OTHER PERSON?
NO !

WHAT IS THE MOST IMPORTANT ISSUE OR PROBLEM FACING YOU TODAY?
I don't really have alot of problems — I'm in college & it's like summer camp b/c I live in my sorority house & basically have fun w/ friends & try not to let my schoolwork get in the way too much

WHAT HABITS DO YOU HAVE THAT WE SHOULD KNOW ABOUT?
I still sleep w/ my teddy bear — when people get mad @ me, my temper either flares or (usually) I just can't stop laughing. I don't sleep a lot very much.

HOW WOULD YOU DESCRIBE YOUR WORST TRAITS?
I'm a terrible procrastinator — which also makes me kind of flaky at times. And I don't have a good sense of direction. At the same time I'm impatient when I set my mind to something.

Casting TARA

<u>Road Rules</u> was my sister's favorite show, but I'd never seen it. These casting people, they showed up at my sorority, and when my roommate met them, she was like, "You have to meet Tara! Oh my God, she'll be perfect for you!" So she came and got me, and I did a little interview and filled out some forms, and that was it. They asked a few of the sorority girls back, but a lot of them dropped out. So it was kind of like they were stuck with me.

WHERE WERE YOU BORN? WHERE DID YOU GROW UP?
I'm a valley girl — born & raised in the San Fernando Valley

DESCRIBE YOUR MOST EMBARRASSING MOMENT.
There are definitely too many to write down — although since I'm always embarrassing myself, it kinda rolls off my back now.

During the trip, I found out that Anne and Roni had to do these grueling interviews where they cried about their families and stuff. For me, the only traumatic point in the interview was when they asked me what music I liked. I told them I dug '80s tunes and stupidly informed them that my roommate and I do a rocking rendition of Rick Springfield's "Jesse's Girl." They asked me to do it right there! I have a terrible singing voice. Like, if you asked me to hum a song, you wouldn't recognize what I'd hummed. Anyway, so I did it. And afterward, the interviewer told me, "Tara, anybody who has that bad of a voice and gets up to sing in front of a million people has got to be okay."

Casting ANNE

I need to see some Action!!

IF YOU COULD ONLY PACK ONE BACKPACK FOR THE TRIP, WHAT WOULD BE IN IT?

Deodorant! Comfortable Shoes, my lucky quarter. ID in case something happens, and something sexy for the hotspots :), and most importantly more than 1 pair of underwear!! :)

TELL US ABOUT SOME PLACES IN THE UNITED STATES YOU HAVE ALWAYS WISHED YOU COULD VISIT AND WHY?
1) Seattle - I hear about it and hear about it
2) South beach - now that looks fun !!
3) Wherever Chris Isaak lives provided he's at home — no fun if he's not there

Okay, I'd just done semifinals, and I thought it'd gone pretty well. But the next night, I'm at work and I get this call. It's the casting people, and they're calling to tell me that the audio on the tape they shot didn't work. They have nothing of me to send to MTV! They told me I needed to get a video camera and spend a day shooting. Well, here it is, this really really busy night at work, and I don't know any-one who's got a video camera—not to mention it's Memorial Day weekend, so everyone's away and most stores are closed. So I finished my shift and started making all these calls. Finally, I found someone with a camera. We spent the day walking around and looking like complete dorks. I put on all these different outfits, talking to the camera the whole time. It was so nerdy!

DESCRIBE YOUR MOST EMBARRASSING MOMENT!!

I have had a bizillion! I have caught my hair in a locked locker, fallen down flights of stairs, wrecked on my dirtbike in front of boys I was trying to impress, had all my underwear stolen (how do you report that?), called boyfriends by the wrong name, fallen down on crowded dance floors — the list goes on and on.....

WHAT HABITS DO YOU HAVE THAT WE SHOULD KNOW ABOUT?

I chew my toenails — kidding. I ask too many questions — people sometimes get bugged. My mom calls it nosey. I call it a thirst for knowledge. I chew on my lip when I think.

WHAT HABITS DO OTHER PEOPLE HAVE THAT YOU SIMPLY CANNOT TOLERATE?

Not at least trying to get along with others — why cause problems; other than that poor personal Hygiene! I just want to yell ⇒ put on some deodorant! Brush your teeth!

HOW DO YOU RATE ON THE FOLLOWING?
(Rate yourself on a 1-10 scale, one being unskilled, and ten very skilled)

ACTIVITY	RATING	COMMENTS
RIDE A BICYCLE	8-9	can't hop rocks — but I can ride!!
RIDE A MOTORCYCLE	7-8	I used to have an YR80 :)
SKI	Watr 2 Snow 1	
RUN A MILE	4-5	I used to run cross country/ tried once — was really bad
SNOWBOARD	1	
ROCK CLIMB	1	
SURF	1	
SPEAK FOREIGN LANGUAGE	4-5	Spanish
FIX A CAR	3-4	my dad made me work on 4 cars
FIX A MOTOR	3-4	
COOK	4	Does mac n cheese count
SEW	3	I can sew a button!!
TIE NAUTICAL KNOTS	1	tried them in girl scouts forgot everything
SAIL A BOAT	1	
SWIM	8	who can't swim? Huh?
FLY	1	
SKYDIVE	1	never done it
WATERSKI	2	oops! I answered above
SCUBA DIVE		
USE A COMPUTER	6-7	I'm in school — Its a must!
DRIVE A BUS		I can drive a tractor does that count?
ROLLERBLADE	5-6	I still fall down things
BUNGEE JUMP	1	
SET UP A TENT	5	If I can remember girl scouts
FIX A FLAT TIRE	9	Now this I can do
READ A MAP	9	Yep — sure can
OTHER SKILLS Balancing a checkbook	8-9	⇐ important
Social Skills	9-10	
touching my tongue to my nose	10	

OK — SO this page makes me feel like I've done NOTHING!!

HOW LONG DOES IT TAKE YOU TO GET READY IN THE MORNING? DO YOU CONSIDER YOURSELF "HIGH MAINTENANCE" OR LOW MAINTENANCE"? WHY?

I think I am BOTH. I take pride in my appearance — I strive to make a good impression — yet you don't get through 5 years of school without learning how to roll out of bed, brush your teeth, comb your hair and GO!!!

DO YOU HAVE A BOYFRIEND OR GIRLFRIEND? HOW DID YOU MEET? HOW LONG HAVE YOU BEEN TOGETHER? WHAT DRIVES YOU CRAZY ABOUT THE OTHER PERSON? WHAT IS THE BEST THING ABOUT THE OTHER PERSON?

Yes, I have a wonderful, sweet girlfriend that gave me her miles so I could come to Michigan to meet with you guys. We've been together on and off for about a year and a half, but seriously (with nothing else going on) since February '97.

The meeting: In early October of last year I was a Senior in High School and had been keeping in touch with a guy in Minneapolis that I met in on a summer trip to Israel. His girlfriend went to school in Madison and so we figured we'd meet halfway in between and spend the night there. The moment I walked in the door of her dorm room I saw this tushie sticking up in the air (a girl was lying on the bed talking on the phone all bunched up in a little ball). What a tush. So I say hello to everyone, but wasn't paying attention to anything except this tush (and what a tush) and it's owners thick New York accent. I whipped out my guitar and everyone started singing in the kitchenette (except this thick New York accented, nicely tushed, ball of a woman lying on the bed). She walked in the kitchen said "What the fu— are you guys doing?" and walked out of the room. That was it. The next morning I walked into the bathroom while she was in the shower, by accident, and she hit me and told me to get out before she kicked my Midwestern booty. I was in love. I'd never met a gorgeous girl with such an attitude. I told her roommate about 200 times in the next week, but nothing came of it until December when Rebecca (my baby) realized what a nice guy I am and invited me to come up and see her.

What drives me crazy? Just that sometimes when I do something that bothers her she doesn't tell me it's bothering her until after she's held it in so long she's ready to explode. Ah, Jamaica, Queens.

The best thing about her is that she's so caring and so thoughtful that she does the sweetest things to turn any day into a great day.

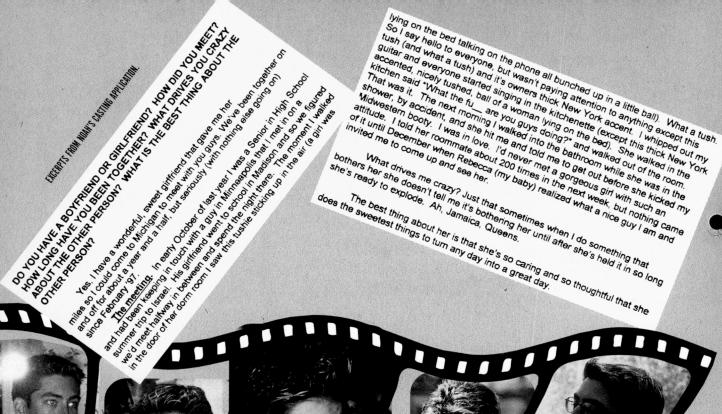

HOW IMPORTANT IS SEX TO YOU? DO YOU HAVE IT ONLY WHEN YOU'RE IN A RELATIONSHIP OR DO YOU SEEK IT OUT AT OTHER TIMES? WHAT'S THE MOST EXCITING/INTERESTING PLACE YOU'VE EVER HAD SEX?

Sex, as itself, is not that important to me. I only have sex while I'm in a relationship, but making love is something very special and very sacred to me. I only have sex while I'm in a relationship, but there was quite an age with one partner it was not really a relationship...it was more of one long, sexual experience. It may have been a relationship, but there was quite an age difference and a lot of obstacles.

OTHER THAN YOUR GIRLFRIEND, WHO IS THE MOST IMPORTANT PERSON IN YOUR LIFE RIGHT NOW? DESCRIBE HIM AND WHY HE IS IMPORTANT.

It's none other than my Big Dad-D-O. Without him I wouldn't be who I am today and know what I know. We've had our differences, but we also have the greatest father/son relationship I know of. We talk every day for about 30 seconds just to see what's up and make sure all is well.

Then I started having problems at school because I was the only guy who would stand up to the bullies and soon no one wanted to be my friend because everyone was afraid they'd have problems too. So instead of hanging out with my friends, I went to work with my dad. It was the best thing that could have happened to me. I learned about life, about all kinds of people,

about business, about standing up for what you believe in, about being a good person, about everything I am today. Now my friends tell me that I could sell ice to Eskimos in the middle of winter and I have nothing to thank for that but experience— and no one to thank for that but my dad. Now, my dad and I just talk often and give each other advice. We don't really spend much time together anymore, but I know that he's there when I need him.

HOW WOULD YOUR GIRLFRIEND FEEL ABOUT YOU LEAVING FOR 10 WEEKS? WOULD YOU BE FAITHFUL?

Even though she gave me the miles, she's still bummed that we can't spend the summer together. When we talked about it she said she's proud of me and excited, too, but she'll miss me lots.

Faithfulness is not even an issue. The answer is 100% yes...why would I ever want to mess up a good thing?

Casting NOAH

IS THIS YOUR FIRST LOVE? IF NOT, DESCRIBE YOUR FIRST LOVE.

No, this is not my first love, but it is my first true love. In the sixth grade I was sure I was in love with Katie _____ I saved up for weeks and bought her one of those heart necklaces that you break in half. I used to dream about going on dates and even getting married (mishoog). The day I gave her the necklace she broke my heart (my real one) because she really liked my best friend Scott and didn't like me anymore.

I was always really confident I'd get picked to do <u>Road Rules</u> but I did have to go through some embarrassing scenarios during the casting process. I was in Detroit for semifinals. The interview was going really well, and then, at the end, they pulled this question out from nowhere. They asked me to name the five Great Lakes. I was like, "What the ????" This is really embarrassing, but for the life of me, I couldn't remember them. I mean, I knew Lake Michigan and one other one, but that was it. Finally, I just admitted I had no idea. Turns out they were just playing with me. That morning, they'd been trying to figure out the names themselves!

Casting RONI

ARE YOU PHYSICALLY FIT?
YES VERY MUCH SO!

WHAT IS THE MOST IMPORTANT ISSUE OR PROBLEM FACING YOU TODAY?
RIGHT NOW...MY MOST IMPORTANT PROBLEM IS DECIDING WHO I'M GOING TO TAKE TO THE PROM. TYPICAL TEENAGE STUFF

ARE YOU PHYSICALLY FIT?
YES VERY MUCH SO!

Photo by Roni's Mom.

I always wanted to be on the show. The second I turned 18, I was like, "Come on, Mom, we gotta make the audition tape for <u>Road Rules</u>!" I wore my pajamas with a jean jacket over them. I made a sign and put it up behind me. It had my name, my address, my phone number, and the words 'Ready, Willing, and Available.'

WHAT HABITS DO YOU HAVE THAT WE SHOULD KNOW ABOUT?
I AM A WILD SLEEPER AND SOMETIMES I SNORE

HOW WOULD YOU DESCRIBE YOUR BEST TRAITS?
I AM A VERY OPEN PERSON WHO IS HONEST FRIENDLY AND UNDERSTANDING

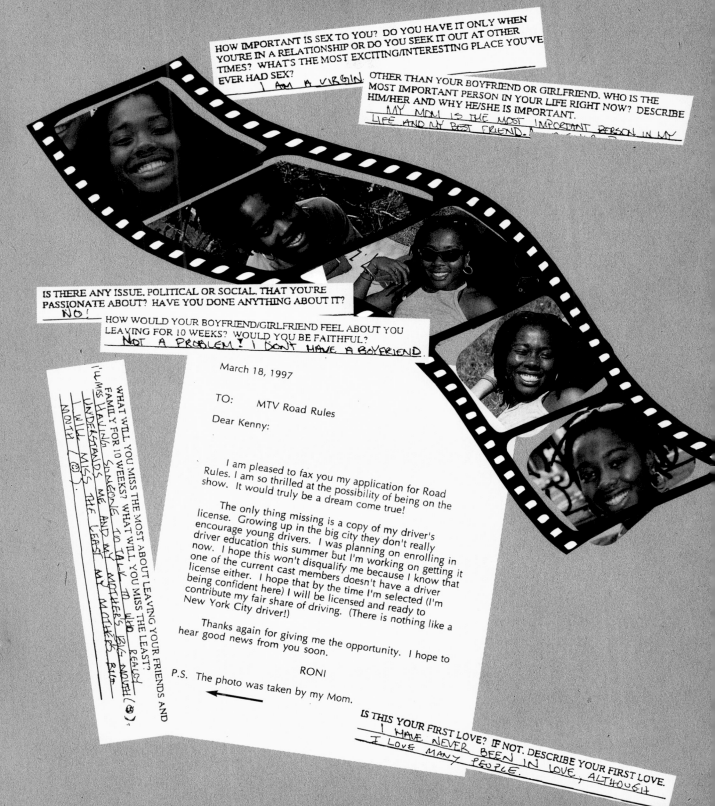

HOW IMPORTANT IS SEX TO YOU? DO YOU HAVE IT ONLY WHEN YOU'RE IN A RELATIONSHIP OR DO YOU SEEK IT OUT AT OTHER TIMES? WHAT'S THE MOST EXCITING/INTERESTING PLACE YOU'VE EVER HAD SEX?
I AM A VIRGIN.

OTHER THAN YOUR BOYFRIEND OR GIRLFRIEND, WHO IS THE MOST IMPORTANT PERSON IN YOUR LIFE RIGHT NOW? DESCRIBE HIM/HER AND WHY HE/SHE IS IMPORTANT.
MY MOM IS THE MOST IMPORTANT PERSON IN MY LIFE AND MY BEST FRIEND.

IS THERE ANY ISSUE, POLITICAL OR SOCIAL, THAT YOU'RE PASSIONATE ABOUT? HAVE YOU DONE ANYTHING ABOUT IT?
NO!

HOW WOULD YOUR BOYFRIEND/GIRLFRIEND FEEL ABOUT YOU LEAVING FOR 10 WEEKS? WOULD YOU BE FAITHFUL?
NOT A PROBLEM! I DON'T HAVE A BOYFRIEND.

WHAT WILL YOU MISS THE MOST ABOUT LEAVING YOUR FRIENDS AND FAMILY FOR 10 WEEKS? WHAT WILL YOU MISS THE LEAST?
I'LL MISS HAVING SOMEONE TO TALK TO WHO REALLY UNDERSTANDS ME AND MY MOTHER'S BIG MOUTH(☺). I WILL MISS THE LEAST MY MOTHER'S BIG MOUTH(☺).

March 18, 1997

TO: MTV Road Rules

Dear Kenny:

I am pleased to fax you my application for Road Rules. I am so thrilled at the possibility of being on the show. It would truly be a dream come true!

The only thing missing is a copy of my driver's license. Growing up in the big city they don't really encourage young drivers. I was planning on enrolling in driver education this summer but I'm working on getting it now. I hope this won't disqualify me because I know that one of the current cast members doesn't have a driver license either. I hope that by the time I'm selected (I'm being confident here) I will be licensed and ready to contribute my fair share of driving. (There is nothing like a New York City driver!)

Thanks again for giving me the opportunity. I hope to hear good news from you soon.

RONI

P.S. The photo was taken by my Mom. ⟵

IS THIS YOUR FIRST LOVE? IF NOT, DESCRIBE YOUR FIRST LOVE.
I HAVE NEVER BEEN IN LOVE, ALTHOUGH I LOVE MANY PEOPLE.

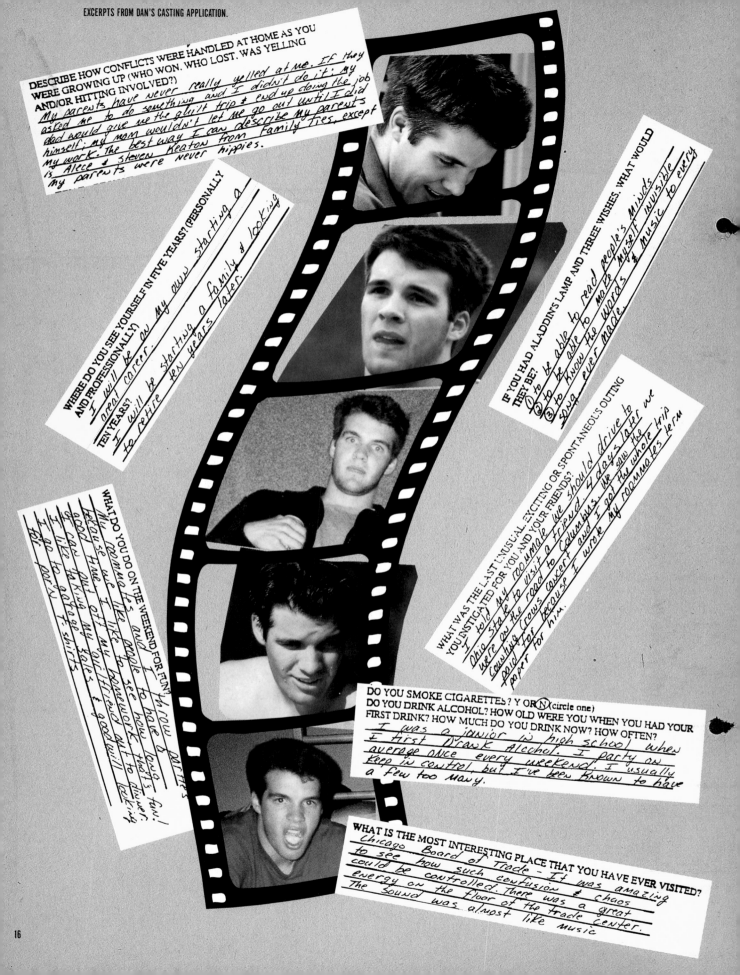

DESCRIBE HOW CONFLICTS WERE HANDLED AT HOME AS YOU WERE GROWING UP (WHO WON. WHO LOST. WAS YELLING AND/OR HITTING INVOLVED?)

My parents have never really yelled at me. If they asked me to do something and I didn't do it; my dad would give me the guilt trip & end up doing the job himself; my mom wouldn't let me go out until I did my work. The best way I can describe my parents is Alece & Steven Keaton from Family Ties, except my parents were never hippies.

WHERE DO YOU SEE YOURSELF IN FIVE YEARS? (PERSONALLY AND PROFESSIONALLY.) TEN YEARS?

I will be on my own starting a great career. I will be starting a family & looking to retire ten years later.

IF YOU HAD ALADDIN'S LAMP AND THREE WISHES, WHAT WOULD THEY BE?

1) to be able to read people's minds
2) to be able to make myself invisible
3) to know the words & music to every song ever made.

WHAT WAS THE LAST UNUSUAL, EXCITING OR SPONTANEOUS OUTING YOU INSTIGATED FOR YOU AND YOUR FRIENDS?

I told my roommate we should drive to Ohio State to visit a friend 4 days later we were on the road to Columbus. We saw the Counting Crows concert and I got the whole trip paid for because I wrote my roommates term paper for him.

WHAT DO YOU DO ON THE WEEKEND FOR FUN?

My roommates and I throw parties because we like people to see how funny we are. But I also like to have a good time. I like taking off my girlfriends & goodwill looking to go to garage sales & goodwill looking for party t-shirts.

DO YOU SMOKE CIGARETTES? Y OR N (circle one)
(N is circled)

DO YOU DRINK ALCOHOL? HOW OLD WERE YOU WHEN YOU HAD YOUR FIRST DRINK? HOW MUCH DO YOU DRINK NOW? HOW OFTEN?

I was a junior in high school when I first drank Alcohol. I party on average once every weekend. I usually keep in control, but I've been known to have a few too many.

WHAT IS THE MOST INTERESTING PLACE THAT YOU HAVE EVER VISITED?

Chicago Board of Trade - It was amazing to see how such confusion & chaos could be controlled. There was a great energy on the floor of the trade center. The sound was almost like music.

Casting DAN

NAME 3 LIVING PEOPLE YOU WOULD LIKE TO MEET AND TELL US WHY.
Marla Aurelas — She's inspirational!
Paul Newman - He's the coolest guy in the world.
Bob Dylan - He's the best poet ever.

DO YOU BELIEVE IN GOD? ARE YOU RELIGIOUS? DO YOU PRACTICE RELIGION?
I believe in God. I'm not religious except for the fact I pray once in a while. I've been raised as a catholic.

I've always been a <u>Real World</u> and <u>Road Rules</u> junkie. Both of those shows, they're just so me. All that talking-about-feelings stuff—it just fits me. I used to watch the marathons thinking how much I wanted to do the show, but for some reason I never thought about making an audition tape. But then, one day, I was just like, "I'm going to do it!" My buddy filmed, and I did stupid things for the camera: I did my Mick Jagger impression and showed off my T-shirt collection. I have about 300 shirts total, but I had to retire a few—they were so old, they were thinner than nylons. Anyway, I guess they thought my T-shirts were cool because I got called for semifinals.

WHAT IS THE BEST THING ABOUT BEING OUT ON YOUR OWN?
I get to take full responsibility for my actions.

Casting JON

DESCRIBE YOUR FANTASY DATE My fantasy date is with Jan Brady from the Brady movies. We'd go sledding and I'd teach her how to skateboard on a skateboard with no wheels. Then we'd make a real goofy movie, just me and her. Then we'd go to my house and watch Japanese cartoons and eat chinese. Then we'd do some serious smooching and maybe go all the way.

WHAT IS YOUR ULTIMATE CAREER GOAL? My ultimate career goal would be to become the next Aaron Spelling. He's the boss. But thats a bit unrealistic. But my other goals are to make it with the band, be a psychologist, be a fashion designer, animator or writer. I also wouldn't mind opening up a cool all ages dance club with weird stuff in it. Making video games is good too.

If you saw The Real World casting special, you know that I wanted to do Real World—Boston and didn't get it. I was pretty crushed. When they asked me if I wanted to be on Road Rules instead, it was like hearing from a girl who just dumped you but has suddenly decided she'd like to be friends. I wanted to do The Real World because the Firehouse was right next to my school, and it'd be free room and board. Going on the road, that was a whole different story. But, I can see why they thought Road Rules would be better for me. I mean, when I went out to L.A. for The Real World finals, I was overwhelmed—and it showed. I was gawking over everything— the supermarket chain called Lucky, the star-shaped chicken strips at Carl's Junior. These things just blew me away. So you can see that I'd be a good guy to have on the road: I've never been anywhere, and everything is new to me.

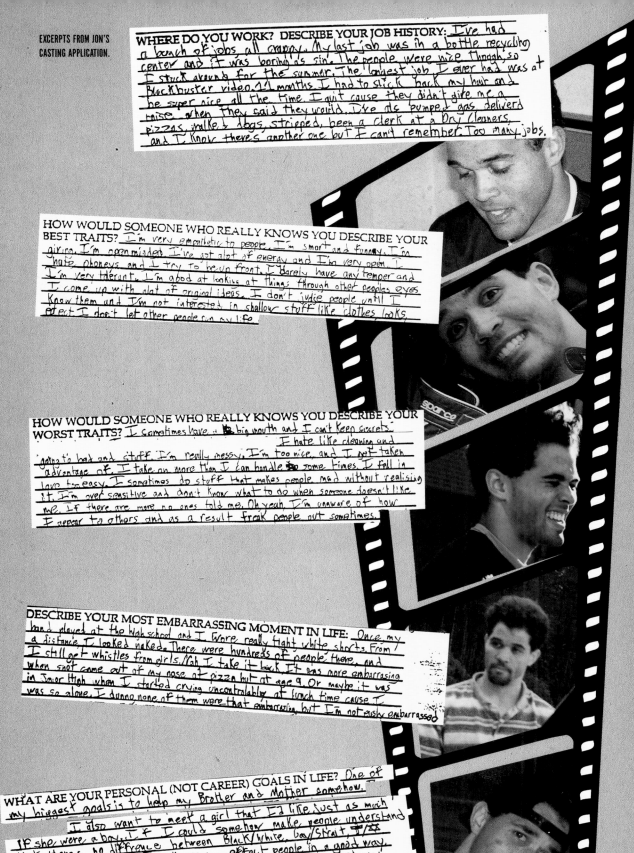

WHERE DO YOU WORK? DESCRIBE YOUR JOB HISTORY: I've had a bunch of jobs all crappy. My last job was in a bottle recycling center and it was boring as sin. The people were nice though, so I stuck around for the summer. The longest job I ever had was at Blockbuster video 11 months. I had to slick back my hair and be super nice all the time. I quit cause they didn't give me a raise, when they said they would. I've also pumped gas, deliverd pizzas, walked dogs, strieped, been a clerk at a Dry Cleaners, and I know there's another one but I can't remember. Too many jobs.

HOW WOULD SOMEONE WHO REALLY KNOWS YOU DESCRIBE YOUR BEST TRAITS? I'm very empathetic to people. I'm smart and funny. I'm giving. I'm openminded. I've got alot of energy and I'm very open. I hate phoneys and I try to be up front. I barely have any temper and I'm very tolerant. I'm good at looking at things through other peoples eyes. I come up with alot of original ideas. I don't judge people until I know them and I'm not interested in shallow stuff like clothes, looks, etc. I don't let other people run my life.

HOW WOULD SOMEONE WHO REALLY KNOWS YOU DESCRIBE YOUR WORST TRAITS? I sometimes have a big mouth and I can't keep secrets. I hate like cleaning and going to bed and stuff. I'm really messy. I'm too nice, and I get taken advantage of. I take on more than I can handle some times. I fall in love too easy. I sometimes do stuff that makes people mad without realising it. I'm over sensitive and don't know what to do when someone doesn't like me. If there are more no ones told me. Oh yeah, I'm unaware of how I appear to others and as a result freak people out sometimes.

DESCRIBE YOUR MOST EMBARRASSING MOMENT IN LIFE: Once my band played at the high school and I wore really tight white shorts. From a distance I looked naked. There were hundreds of people there. I still get whistles from girls. Yeah I take it back. It was more embarrassing when snot came out of my nose at pizza hut at age 9. Or maybe it was in Junior High when I started crying uncontrolably at lunch time cause I was so alone. I dunno none of them were that embarrassing, but I'm not easily embarrassed.

WHAT ARE YOUR PERSONAL (NOT CAREER) GOALS IN LIFE? One of my biggest goals is to help my Brother and Mother somehow. I also want to meet a girl that I'd like just as much if she were a boy. If I could somehow make people understand that theres no difference between Black/White, Gay/Strait, I'd feel damn good. I really wanna effect people in a good way. I also want to have alot of money, and to some day meet my favorite artists and directors. But most importantly, I wanna have Kids and bring them up good.

19

Cameo Appearances By
DAN'S family, NOAH'S family, RONI'S mom, stock-car driver DAN KITCH,
the ROYAL CANADIAN MOUNTED POLICE, the MANDARI
INDIAN RESERVATION tribes,

Guide to

ANNE

DAN

JON

With Special Appearances by

JEN as Jon's returning love • "I DON'T KNOW" as Tara's fallback guy
The Cast of • <u>ROAD RULES IV</u> as the old-timers and • The <u>REAL WORLD ALL-STARS</u> as the competition

RACHEL	**NATASCHA**	**DR. TIM**	**SEAN**
as Dan's jilted yet noble ex	as Noah's babe on the side	as Anne's personal physician	as the Lumberjack Stud

the physicians and nurses of DETROIT RECEIVING HOSPITAL, the employees of CINNEBURST GUM, four wayward COWS, six dehydrated HORSES....

ROAD RULES

NORTHERN TRAIL

NOAH

RONI

TARA

And Introducing ... HUFF, PUFF, and BLOW THE HOUSE DOWN

Co-Starring...
THIRD EYE BLIND • RICHARD KARN'S celebrity golfers
DANIEL BALDWIN, SAMUEL L. JACKSON, and ROLLIE FINGERS
• The WORLD WRESTLING FEDERATION'S Own CHAZ and
THRASHER • The CHICAGO BEARS rookies • Several pro
hockey players, along with MONTREAL'S very own RINK RATS

ABDUCTED!

RONI: About a week before the trip, the casting people called me up. They told me that they'd narrowed down the group of finalists to ten, and out of that group, five would go on the road. They wouldn't tell me if I'd definitely been picked, but they instructed me to pack my bags and be ready to leave the next weekend. That's what they did to all of us—told us that we might be going, but we might not—very nerve-wracking.

CAST MEMBER	TIME/PLACE OF ABDUCTION	SPECIAL CIRCUMSTANCES
Anne	AM/Her home	Nursing hangover
Roni	PM/The prom	High heels
Dan	AM/Bagel shop	Hanging with mom
Jon	AM/His home	In the shower
Noah	PM/His home	Saw them coming
Tara	AM/Sorority house	Wasted

The one suspicious thing is that they sent me a huge backpack full of stuff. I thought, "It'd be really bad to get all this stuff, then have to give it back if you didn't get chosen." But it turns out they knew who was going to be picked the whole time. They were playing a trick on us.

I really didn't know I was going to get on the show until Jake and Kalle from Season IV showed up at my prom. That was the craziest thing—they showed up at my prom—all these crew people and Jake and Kalle wearing ski masks—and the chaperone wouldn't let them in. He was so freaked-out, he called my mom to inform her that people in army fatigues were attempting to abduct her child.

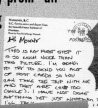

RONI AND HER PROM DATE

Get acquainted...bungee style!

Number of castmates: 6
Number of castmates who liked KALLE: 6
Number of castmates who liked JAKE: 2
What JON packed: ukulele, rubber-dart gun,
MC Hammer doll, dragon ball toys, duct tape

FIRST IMPRESSIONS

FROM ANNE'S DIARY

Tara - sunny blonde from
'LA funny, a little
sarcastic - liked her.
(UCLA)

Noah - a little 😊 on the strange
side - plays guitar
great eyes very skinny
but good style 😊
? school

Roni - cute chick - sitting
next to me I was peeking
from the blindfold and
thinking who is this girl → ?
dreds to her shoulders
all business with the
computer (LOVES $ THE COMPUTER)
plays with it a lot
(Performing Arts)

Dan - last member to
add the to the group
nice - good looking reminds
me alot of Paul Steinberg!
(Jace looks) has a cute
laugh

John - Nicest guy in the
world he's given me
his Ray Bans - crazy! But
I think its really sweet
(was bummed about my
sunglasses and he just
gave me his!) How sweet
concerned about his self
esteem though. He puts himself
down quite a bit. He's really
a good guy odd but good.

DAN: When I first met Anne, I was like, "WHAT A TOTAL PRISS!"

NOAH: I showed up expecting more worldly, more MTV-type people, but what I found was just a bunch of kids like me.

TARA: When they told us we were going to be the first <u>Road Rules</u> with six people not five, I thought they were pulling something on us. I thought we were going to have to travel with some kind of pet, like maybe a monkey. It turned out to be Dan.

Jon: The people are not what I expected them to be. They're all normal!

NOAH: I really wanted to beat the Islands cast. Right off the bat, that Jake was rude to me. He told me he noticed that I was one person on camera and another person off, and I better watch out for that. I was thinking, "Dude, you don't even know me!"

MISSION

Rev up, <u>Road Rulers</u>! It's time to show the Islands cast that their time is past! Become speed racers on the stock-car runway.

The Whisper Twins

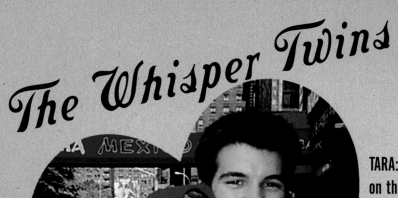

TARA: Dan told me he liked me on the third day of the trip. It was off camera. Really, the cameras couldn't keep up with me and Dan. We stayed up until four A.M. every night, whispering in bed. That's why Anne called us "the whisper twins."

TARA: Dan's a really complex person. You can tell in his poetry. It's very honest. All the things he thinks about but can't express are in it. He's so analytical and can express himself so clearly on paper.

Poetry Helps me when I think I can't see -
I have a lot of words But I know they're not me -
If I said I was a liar I know you would believe - If I came to you with a problem I know I would deceive -
The whole question of truth has been raised too much -
The whole question of being relies on such - In a time when feeling shallow isn't a choice - I have but one utensil to be my true voice - If I could explain the flow I feel - I know my worries would reveal th...

Being full of a feeling that I know
Isn't rage - Makes me spit out words
to fill one more page - Pleasant thoughts
are nice but they often times drain - A true
bearer of souls who is good at this game -
Walls are useless when you know
what's inside - Criminals are the only ones
that who I can abide - I sit beneath a
mountain of things I've created - Not one
of the rocks is something I've hated -
Now, my mountain is something that I admire
The challenge to climb it will test my desire.
I'm a young boy now so I ~~think~~
Know I can make it - But will the people
around me sit and take it - It feels like
I push people off my own peak - only to
realize that I am the ~~we~~ weak - falling
down the side; I am not afraid - It's hitting
the bottom that my hands have laid.
I'm tired of thoughts that do me no
good - They're only part of reasons I think
I should - Why am I strange about the
things I preach - I wish I was the
one my words could teach - I feel
like I should ~~~~~
squeakin' - If I'm so put together
why can't I relate - To the things in
my life I know I'll always hate -
If you feel like you know me there's
a lot you can't ___ If you feel
like you own me - ___ ___ cau_
I'M M___

ROAD RULES VANDALISM
Case #001

NOAH: Our horns got stolen. These creeps left a ransom note that said: "Meet me at Elliot's at 3:30 P.M. if you want your skull back." We scoped out the city, found a place called Elliot's, and when we got there, there was another note telling us to go somewhere else. We're furious at this point, but we go. Finally, we find this girl who says she's got them, and that they were given to her by a bunch of guys in ski masks. I don't know if that was true or not. Sounds pretty fishy, but we got them back.

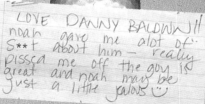

LOVE DANNY BALDWIN!!
noah gave me alot of
s**t about him - really
pissed me off the guy is
great and noah may be
just a little jealous :)

ANNE'S DIARY

MISSION

Put your polo shirts on!
Become chatty caddies as you
go clubbin' with the stars!

ANNE

ANNE'S IDEAL ROAD RULES CAST:

KIT from Season One, CHRISTIAN and TIMMY from Season Two, MICHELLE from Season Three, and ERIKA from Season Four.

ANNE'S ADVICE TO FUTURE ROAD RULERS

ANNE: Be yourself! Even if you know you're coming off like a bi**h and a cry baby, it doesn't matter. If that's who you are, it's okay. Don't try and be fake, because people know when you're being fake. And if you're yourself, people will love you.

WHAT'S ANNE GOING TO BE WHEN SHE GROWS UP?

DAN: Hopefully, with Dr. Tim.
JON: Talk-show host
RONI: Something with a Ph.D. or an M.D.
TARA: An accountant
NOAH: In grad school

ANNE: Watching Road Rules is like watching a home video. I don't really regret how I behaved, but still, watching it is kind of an eye-opener. It's like, "God, I'm a dork."

It's weird how many people watch the show. I was shopping at the mall the other day, and these girls were following me and giggling. Finally, I confronted them: "Why are you laughing at me? Did I sit in something?"

My family loves watching it. They think it's so me. Of course, they didn't really like seeing me kiss that Brandon guy. My mom was like, "How can I tell people to watch the show when you're there looking like a hussy?" She was joking, of course.

RONI: Anne's a sweetheart!

DAN: Next to Tara, Anne was my closest friend on the trip. It took us a while to bond, for me to really get to know her, but once we did, there was no turning back.

TARA: Anne was my confidante. I'd like to be more like her, more attuned to people's problems, more sensitive. Sometimes she knows just what to say.

JON: When Anne and I connected, I'd get a funny little feeling inside. I calculated that my crushes on Anne would last somewhere between 25 and 40 minutes each. I'd feel all this nice stuff, but then she'd get all cranky and ornery, and I'd be over it. And I didn't like all her fashion talk!

NOAH: Anne was my best friend on the trip, no doubt. I hated feeling like sometimes she couldn't look me in the eye.

DESIGNED BY ROAD RULES CAST

27

TARA: I was definitely the messiest, definitely.

NOAH: The Winnie was so nasty, I felt dirty for nine weeks straight.

THE WINNIE

Yo ! These past two or three days have been hell ! I hate the Winnie with a passion. I have never met such nasty people in my life. Tare is the nastiest of them all. It is like my words to them go in one ear and out the other. I asked them just to clean up after themselves after they take off their clothes. But no, they are too nasty for that. Tara will pull s**t out and never pick it up. I don't think she's ever cleaned in her life. I hate the fact that I made this big speech about cleaning and the Winnie is back to its normal nasty self.

FROM RONI'S JOURNAL

WHAT'S THE DIRTIEST THING ABOUT 'BAGO LIVING?

ANNE: The toilet overflowing into my clothes and shoes! Second to that, the flies that collected in there after we did livestock missions. They would not get out!

RONI: The sink in the kitchen that was full of molded dishes.

JON: The stench of sweat from our beds. We had no sheets.

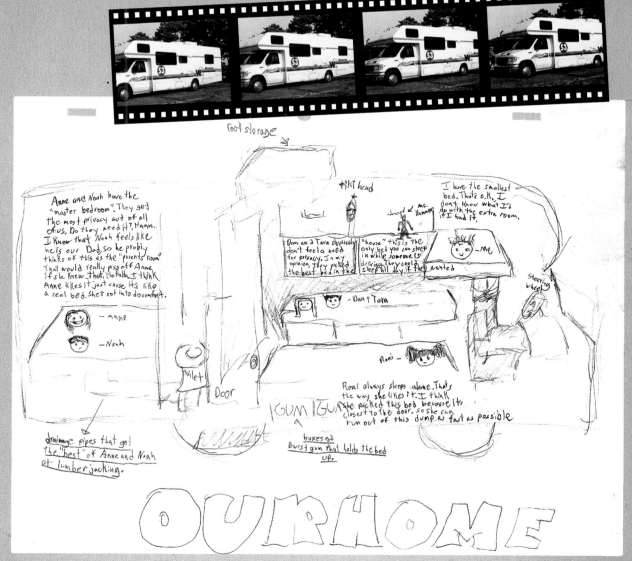

JON'S RENDITION OF THE WINNIE

ROAD RULES VANDALISM Case #002

> DAMN! THE WINNIE GOT BROKEN INTO! I LOST EVERYTHING! EVERYTHING!

RONI'S JOURNAL

LOCK UP!
ANNE: Tara and I were kind of shocked when we found this out: Roni locks her backpack. In the Winnebago, she locks it! There are six of us on this trip, and we're going to have to rely on one another and trust one another, and there's not a lot of "This is mine, that's yours." This whole trip is about trust.

Anne & Noah

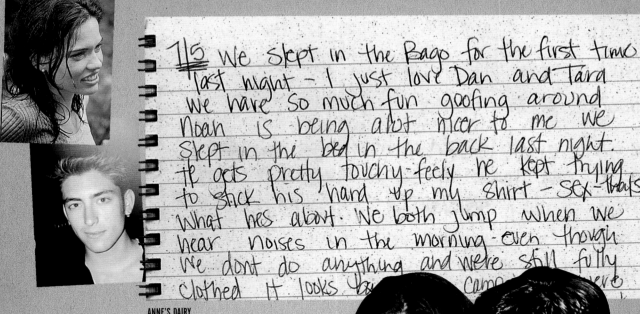

1/5 We slept in the Bago for the first time last night - I just love Dan and Tara. We have so much fun goofing around Noah is being alot nicer to me we slept in the bed in the back last night. He gets pretty touchy-feely he kept trying to stick his hand up my shirt - sex-thats what hes about. We both jump when we hear noises in the morning - even though we dont do anything and were still fully clothed. It looks ba_____ cam_____ ____

ANNE'S DAIRY

Anne: "Noah and I, we just had this total scandal going on. At the beginning of the trip, we got really close. We'd snuggle and do some kiss-on-the-face things."

Day 7

All I can do to explain this day is list the sucky and not sucky events. Sucky first.

1 Our tire blew causing mucho stress
2 We had to blow $150 on totally low-budg. video equp.
3 Anne kept crying. Her pain is my pain, I guess
4 I lost Zero, my 3rd favorite Yoy
5 We met the band 3rd Eye Blind and they were pin heads. Well not really, but the singer was.
6 My travel mates actually started to get on my nerves a little. VERY BAD. I thought it would never happen
7 I had to drive. I hate the Winniebago.
8 We didn't leave Scarlette. I'm so ant-sea!
9 I still have a goatee. 10 I miss Jen.

Now for the Not Sucky

1 I litle Ramen Noodles! Yum Yum!

Jon

FROM JON'S DIARY

MISSION

Film a Public Service Announcement about teen suicide to the tune of Third Eye Blind's song, "Jumper."

ANNE: After all the hell of the PSA mission, I'm really glad I did it. It really meant something to me—even though it was really difficult.

NOAH: I read Anne's Diary. "What the Hell???" That diary, she wrote it as a self-defense mechanism. I disagree with 90% of it. I was never interested in Anne. I just liked to cuddle. And the truth is that when we were sleeping together or out drinking, she made a lot of passes at me.

1/7 Noah and I are getting way too involved hes being really aggressive and I'm really annoyed with it — woke up and its not so much the cuddling anymore — he is just aggressive and I'm really not OK with him — I had a very angry day towards him — he can be such an ass during the day and then he expects to cuddle at night — we really did not do

Thank god, Tara and I played catch she says that dan thinks I want Noah — I really am hating the things that people are assuming — (1) I'm a priss (2) I'm a b**ch (3) I want Noah (4) I cant handle myself — I'm just

ANNE'S DAIRY

ANNE: Noah thinks he's irresistible. Really, whatever. If he can't fess up to truth, that's his problem. I let him read my diary and now I regret it. There's trust for you.

MISSION

Hit the Mats! It's Wrestlemania, Road Rules–style!

Chaz & Thrasher's Nicknames for The Road Rulers

ANNE = NANCY
RONI = QUEEN LATIFAH
TARA = STINKY
DAN = STUDLY
JON = SPANKY
NOAH = PANSY

31

ROAD RULES V: THE LOST EPISODES

PIKE STREET FISH MARKET

DAN: For the fish job, I wasn't hungover. Actually, I'd never gone to sleep. I was just coming off my buzz.

JON: You don't see this on the show, but after being up all night doing the Third Eye Blind mission, we had to wake up at the crack of dawn to work at a fish market. Except for me and Roni, everyone else was hungover. It was brutal. I was an oyster stacker. Roni manned the fish-catching duties. Anne hosed stuff down. Tara and Dan shoveled fish. And Noah, with his anti-authority attitude, he got booted to the cooler, where he had to skin fish. Noah was rude, so he was given the worst job possible.

MISSION

Get suited up and stand up straight! You're now a member of the Royal Canadian Mounted Police.

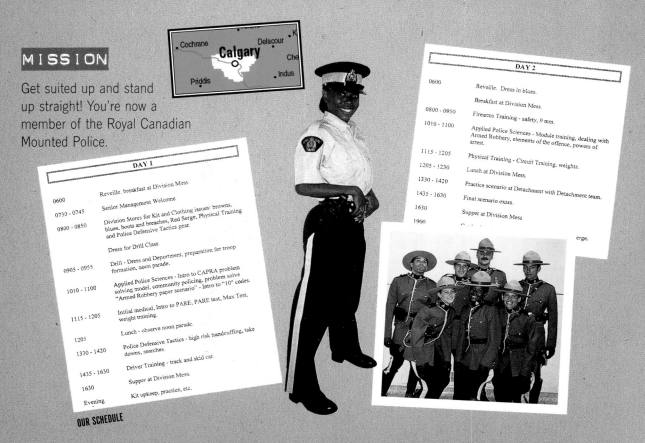

DAY 1

0600	Reveille, breakfast at Division Mess
0730 - 0745	Senior Management Welcome
0800 - 0850	Division Stores for Kit and Clothing issues: browns, blues, boots and breaches, Red Serge, Physical Training and Police Defensive Tactics gear.
	Dress for Drill Class
0905 - 0955	Drill - Dress and Deportment, preparation for troop formation, noon parade.
1010 - 1100	Applied Police Sciences - Intro to CAPRA problem solving model, community policing, problem solve "Armed Robbery paper scenario" - Intro to "10" codes.
1115 - 1205	Initial medical, Intro to PARE, PARE test, Max Test, weight training.
1205	Lunch - observe noon parade.
1330 - 1420	Police Defensive Tactics - high risk handcuffing, take downs, searches.
1435 - 1630	Driver Training - track and skid car.
1630	Supper at Division Mess.
Evening	Kit upkeep, practice, etc.

OUR SCHEDULE

DAY 2

0600	Reveille. Dress in blues.
	Breakfast at Division Mess.
0800 - 0950	Firearms Training - safety, 9 mm.
1010 - 1100	Applied Police Sciences - Module training, dealing with Armed Robbery, elements of the offence, powers of arrest.
1115 - 1205	Physical Training - Circuit Training, weights.
1205 - 1230	Lunch at Division Mess.
1330 - 1420	Practice scenario at Detachment with Detachment team.
1435 - 1630	Final scenario exam.
1630	Supper at Division Mess
1900	

SHOVELING MANURE FOR CASH

NOAH'S DIARY

* MANURE

Before we left Calgary, we were given an opportunity to work for some money to replace our stolen clothes—well, actually, Roni, Tara, and Dan's stolen clothes. But we all worked—well, actually some of us worked. I couldn't believe that I was shovelling manure to help Roni, Tara, and Dan get their clothes back and I had to listen to Tara bitch and moan about how she didn't want to work and that she wanted to give up. I really thought I was doing something for the good of the group, but Tara made me feel as if I was working for nothing. she's so closed minded and immature about a lot of things, to and I'm sure

Day 15

Noah thinks this trip is boring. I say he's nuts.
Sure, we shoveled Cow Poo-Poo for 3 hrs today,
and didn't do much else, but come on. These people
are so interesting. It's spell binding. It's almost all
I think about. Here's a diagram
see, It's so coplicated it doesn't
even make sense. I don't care
for Roni, but she makes eyes at

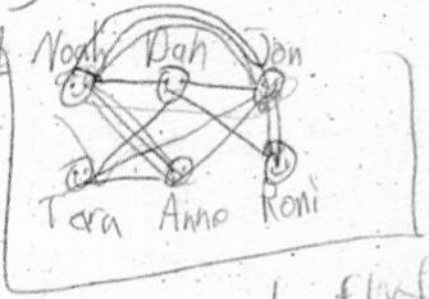
Noah
Dan
Jon
Tara
Anne
Roni

Noah and Dan, Dan likes Terra, but Terra gets flirty
with me. But she defintly like Dan Best. I love/hate
Noah, but not very strongly either way. Noah and Anne
are constantly on the verge of beating the snot out of
each other or sucking face. Anne and Tara are best
buddies but for how long?. Roni seems to think Tera
and Anne suck. Dan likes everyone, or so it appears.
But deep down, does he respect everyone?. Who knows.
Theres so much left to see, to feel, and to find out.
And then theres the little matter of the missions,
the traveling, and the prize. How the [illegible]
could Noah be bored I just don't get it.

Jon

JON'S DIARY

ANNE: Shoveling horse manure was the most disgusting thing I ever did. Every time you shoveled it, you got a massive whiff of urine and ammonia. Then, of course, Dan found a little mouse corpse, which he threw at me. I was sure it was stuck in my coveralls or my shoe.

Tara was actually losing it more than I was. You could see tears welling in her eyes; she hated it, she hated it. She felt degraded and terrible, and why should she have to work so hard to get her stuff back?

7/8

Horse manure! Car won't start! Got hives! Got lost! Crashed Bago! —Tara's amazing day!

TARA'S DIARY

DREAMS

JON'S FREAKED-OUT DREAM #1
I had a dream about meeting all these other cast members in a giant hotel room. I didn't recognize any faces, but they were all cast members from different <u>Real World</u> and <u>Road Rules</u> shows. I had a strong feeling that I did not fit in, and that everyone else felt the same way. Somehow, I ended up in a room that was decorated in a Victorian manner. It was very small, maybe 8 feet by 8 feet. Tara was in the room. She was alone and happy. I walked over to her to talk, and things were as relaxed and friendly as always. All of a sudden, we were kissing passionately. It felt like an eruption. I didn't know if I could stop. Why it ended, I don't know. It was like someone switched a light on and then off. I felt so guilty, yet happy. not sure if I like the fact that I had this dream.

JON'S FREAKED-OUT DREAM #2
I had another dream about kissing Tara, except this time it was much more passionate. I pushed my lips hard against hers, kind of the way Jimmy Stewart kisses Donna Reed in <u>It's a Wonderful Life</u> when he first tells her he loves her, except with an open mouth. I don't know why I have these dreams. I find Tara attractive, yet I don't feel very close to her. I feel distant.

TARA: Jon doesn't like people getting together. He really has a problem with it. His bunk was above mine and Dan's. We'd be necking a little bit, and we'd look up, and there would be Jon staring at us in this menacing way. That's probably why he had those dreams about me, because he watched me like that. I told him it made me uncomfortable. I have no idea what his deal is. If we don't get together, how does he benefit? And it wasn't only us he did it to. He did it to Noah and Anne. when they were meeting people.

RUNNING

I
N
T
E
R
F
E
R
E
N
C
E

1052 MAN!

DAN AND TARA'S PRIVATE CODES
1010=Jon's running interference
1052=I love you
1053=Blechh!
10301=Oh God, right there!

JON: I never tried to screw Dan and Tara over. They're just paranoid. I admit, I tried to break up Noah's hookups with girls, but that's because I was protecting the girls. But, Dan and Tara, I never did anything to them—at least, not on purpose. I will admit that I was clueless. I'd be asking them if they wanted to talk, when maybe what they wanted to do was fool around. I have nothing against affection. Honestly.

Song: "You Stupid Cow"
Written by: Jon
Sung a la Sinatra

You are a pain in my ass
A pain in my ass go away
And you too, you stupid cow
It's time for you to pay!

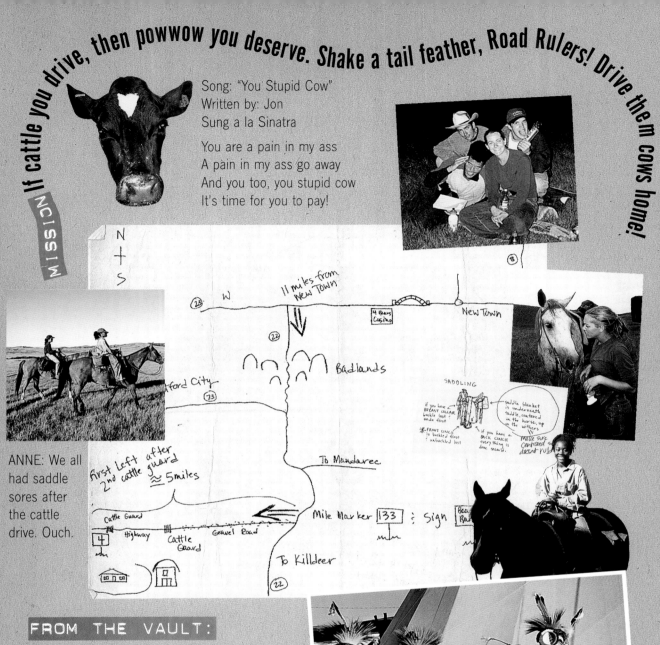

ANNE: We all had saddle sores after the cattle drive. Ouch.

FROM THE VAULT:

ROAD RULES V: THE LOST EPISODES

SWEATIN'

RONI: You don't see it on the show, but when we were at the Indian reservation, they had us go into a sweat lodge. It's this really spiritual experience, sweating. I'm not a churchgoer, but I'm very spiritual. I believe in God, and I'm pretty open to everything. But when the heat first hit me, I got scared. I thought it would just be unbearable. It wasn't though. You just sit back, and it's so peaceful.

THE CAST GETS INDIAN NAMES.

ANNE = YELLOW CORN WOMAN
RONI = BRINGER OF SAGE
JON = RIDES THE HORSE
NOAH = TWO FEATHERS
DAN = EAGLE WING
TARA = RED CORN WOMAN

RONI

RONI: I had a hard time opening up to my cast. There was no one I completely clicked with. I was really different from all of them. Before them, I'd never been to the suburbs, I'd never watched <u>Seinfeld</u>. I really wish there'd been another African-American on the trip. I know Jon's of mixed race, but it's different somehow.

Road Rules was my first time on my own. I turned into a totally different person. My mom babies me, and on the trip I was all on my own. I had to take care of myself.

RONI'S IDEAL ROAD RULES CAST:

CARLOS from Season One, EFFIE from Season Two, ANTOINE and BELOU from Season Three, ERIKA from Season Four, and NOAH from our season. (I'd just like to see that! They'd probably all kill one another!)

WHAT'S RONI GOING TO BE WHEN SHE GROWS UP?

JON: President
ANNE: She'll start go-go dancing schools all over the world!
TARA: A dancer or a banker
NOAH: In Broadway shows
DAN: In politics. But she'll be honest. She'll keep it real.

The places we went, they were all so different to me. I'm used to seeing a mix of different people. On the road, I was often the only black person. We'd be walking down the street, and I'd hear someone whisper: "How does she get her hair like that?"

You know what I missed, being on <u>Road Rules</u>? Being attracted to someone. The whole time, the only people I thought were hot were two of the Chicago Bears rookies. I bet people watching the show think there's something wrong with me—it looks like I'm not into romance at all.

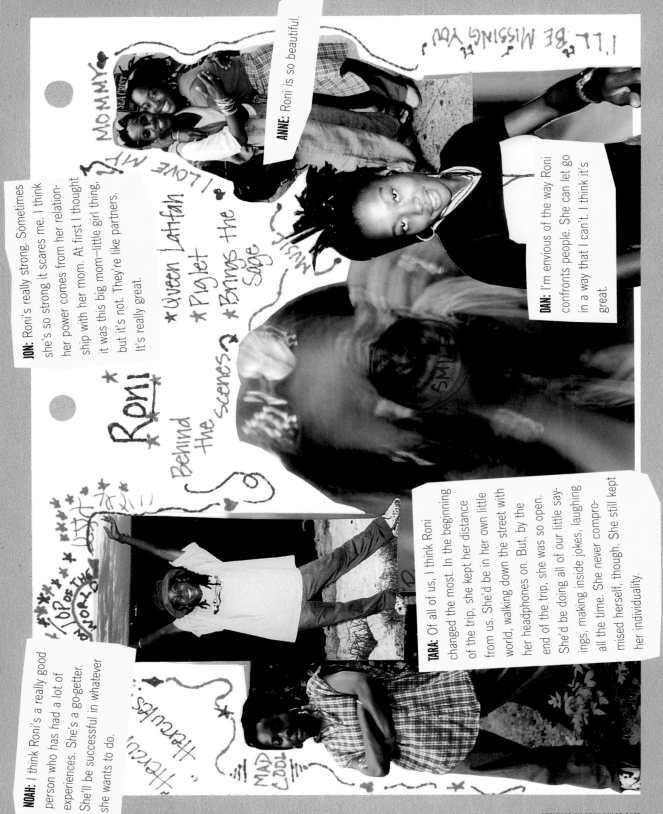

I'LL BE MISSING YOU.

ANNE: Roni is so beautiful.

MOMMY

I LOVE MY

Queen Latifah
*Piglet
*Brings the Sage

JON: Roni's really strong. Sometimes she's so strong it scares me. I think her power comes from her relationship with her mom. At first I thought it was this big mom—little girl thing, but it's not. They're like partners. It's really great.

DAN: I'm envious of the way Roni confronts people. She can let go in a way that I can't. I think it's great.

Roni

Behind the scenes

SMIL

TOP OF THE WORLD

MAD COOL

#Hercules #Hercule

NOAH: I think Roni's a really good person who has had a lot of experiences. She's a go-getter. She'll be successful in whatever she wants to do.

TARA: Of all of us, I think Roni changed the most. In the beginning of the trip, she kept her distance from us. She'd be in her own little world, walking down the street with her headphones on. But, by the end of the trip, she was so open. She'd be doing all of our little sayings, making inside jokes, laughing all the time. She never compromised herself, though. She still kept her individuality.

DESIGNED BY ROAD RULES CAST

Going Home to DAN'S

AND MEET EAGLE WING'S EX!

NOAH VS. DAN

NOAH: Dan pulled some d**k moves when we were at his house in Minneapolis. He made it seem like he and his ex-girlfriend Rachel were really broken up when they weren't. He was already fooling around with Tara when we got to Minneapolis, but he still had Rachel going, too. One day when we were there, I was playing piano and I saw Dan and Rachel totally hooking up—not hard-core, but making out, kind of.

> 12 AM
> I'm kind of sketching out right now about Dan. I guess I always do when we don't get a chance to talk, just b/c I'm so used to talking about EVERYTHING w/ him.
> But he was really bummed all day b/c he talked to Rachel last night & I feel really bad for him b/c I feel like he needs someone else here besides me that he can talk to about this stuff. The whole thing is really hard for him b/c he's trying so hard to do everything right w/ her & its a no-win situation b/c any way it happens, she's going to be hurt.
> Things have been getting more intense w/ us in the couple of days before we came here. I feel really close to him, I hate to see him upset. Also, I ~~fe~~el responsible for Rachel being so ~~up~~set & for ~~bot~~ everything being hard on ~~bo~~th of them.

TARA'S DIARY

DAN: I'm really pissed off about Noah saying Rachel and I kissed. Rachel and I went out for two years, and things were really complicated, and although we were definitely broken up, I was trying to comfort her. I mean, I'd totally broken her heart. I don't remember kissing her, but I asked her about it, and she says we did a little. I was really drunk. I don't remember anything from that night. But I just can't believe Noah would say that. I'm so mad. I never say anything about his hookups. Maybe because his attitude toward girls is so disgusting, I get too grossed-out to talk about it. But forget it, when the time comes, I will talk about it!

NOAH was okay.

ANNE was my favorite. She looks like Nancy Kerrigan, but she's more like Jenny McCarthy. If I were going to have a crush on one of them, it would be Anne.

TARA, she was pretty quiet, but that's because of the whole Rachel situation.

As far as that goes, RACHEL wasn't really herself that weekend. She was so nervous. That was the longest she and Danny had been apart. She wasn't into the cameras at all. They miked her, but she got really upset and threw the mike off. She'd be trying to talk to her friends and the cameras would be in her face, and everything she was saying was being recorded. She got really pissed.

FROM THE COMPOSITION NOTEBOOK OF...
Dan's Little Brother, Dave

Having <u>Road Rules</u> at my house was so cool! Everyone was so friendly; it was like my brother had known them his whole life. The people in my town got pretty into it. All the neighbors brought over food, and all the girls kept trying to be on camera. Everywhere the cameras were, these girls went. They were doing anything to get on the show—like scamming on Noah, Danny, and Jon.

JON performed "Ladies' Night" for us, but only after we paid him. He kept saying, "No, no, no," but when everyone offered money, he had to say yes.

RONI I really liked, but I didn't see her that much. She seemed kind of on the outside.

RACHEL TALKS BACK!

RACHEL: The episode was just NOT how it was. It makes me look like I'm this helpless little girl holding onto some nonexistent high school romance. That's not what it was like. I knew it was over. I wanted us to be friends, that's all. The truth is I felt good after Dan's visit. I was really happy and sure we'd be friends. Somehow, the episode makes me look like I'm really bitter—I wasn't that way, at all.

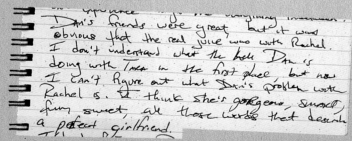

TARA: I don't have anything against Rachel, but I don't want to be her best friend, either.

NOAH'S DIARY

Loggin'! Spelunkin'! Ax throwin'! Lumber jack it up, Road Rulers!

I'M A LUMBERJACK, I'M OKAY!.

FROM THE SCORECARD OF LUMBERJACK SPORTS CHAMP AND THE REAL WORLD ALUM, SEAN...

"A Lumberjack Named Sean."

Written and performed by Noah. Back-up vocals by Jon and Dan

Yeah, I'm a Lumberjack, I'm a Lumberjack, that's what I am

SEAN: When I first met Dan, I didn't like him too much. I thought he was just too hard-core all-American. He and Tara had a cute relationship, though. She was athletic and sweet. Anne was cute, too, a little bit whiny, though. People always ask me if we fooled around. She's a hottie, but, no, we didn't. Jon, he was so weird. He just didn't say anything. He's really not caught up in any of this masculinity stuff. I guess I admire that. Roni wasn't talkative, either. She seemed to really be on the outside of the group.

As for Noah, he and I are both from Wisconsin, so we talked cheese. I was pulling for him to win because he wanted to so bad. But, really, he had no skill.

ANNE: Sean looked so much cuter than he did on The Real World. I was just like, "Whoa."

Here's what Anne thinks about Lumberjacks:

Well, I never met a man who looks so good and I never met a man who looked so fine and I like to see him climb up and down that big tree over there that looks like a pine.

He's a lumberjack

Well, you'd think a lumberjack would be named something like Bob or James or Billy or Joe, but this one here, he's called Sean. And Sean's all right, but you know what I'm saying about the way Anne looks at him, that's why I'm singing this song.

He's a lumberjack, yes, a lumberjack, that's what Sean is.

BRANDON: The Real Deal

did alot more than I did — I was
or still am PISSED OFF — I called
him — said I heard etc he denied
of course but then I just simply
stated "It shows a serious lack
of judgement on your part to spread
rumors I have way more power
to ruin you than you do to ruin
me — the only thing I have to do
all day long is sit around and
talk about people — on national
television. I hear stuff and suddenly
you have a steriod probem then
I hear more stuff and you have
sores" he got really upset and
was scared that I'm saying stuff
so I said "you'll just have to watch

ANNE'S DIARY

ANNE: In Wisconsin, I met one of Noah's friends, this guy Brandon. We kissed a little, but no big deal, just fun and whatever. Well, afterward Noah told me he was telling people we'd done much more than we did. I was livid.

MI$$ION

Bubble, bubble, you've got money trouble! Strap on your hair nets, and chew on this! It's Cinneburst to the rescue!

MISSION

Break out the tunes, Road Rulers and rookies. It's the First Annual Chicago Bears Kabong Show!

what it meant. ♡ I was going home (chez
moi), but not right away. The whole concept
of working in a gum factory was really cool
to me — especially the fact that we
could have all the gum we wanted! If I
was 10, my life would have been complete. The
day was great, except for when Anne and TARA
won $500 and decided they would buy each
of us something little and blow the rest on
themselves. I don't really give a f**k
about money, but on the road money is
the only thing that gets you by because it's
the only way to eat and live comfortably.
HAD I known Anne & TARA were going
to be so selfish and say s**t like,

"Well it's our money" — I'd have won the
f***ing contest. It never was a thought
in my mind that the money was not going
to be "group money". I just couldn't believe
the situation. It was just one example of why
TARA & Anne annoyed me so much. I mean,
we were totally pressed for cash and I
knew that in the weeks to come we'd go
broke, and that Anne & TARA would either
end up wearing the money (like overalls) or
drinking it.

NOAH'S DIARY

AT THE SIGN. THE SIGN SAYS "KEEP BACK"
DO NOT FEED THE BEARS 'CAUSE OF ALL NFL
NOT A SINGLE TEAM DARES IN THE
TO STAND UP, TO TRY TO MAKE A PLAY
EVEN RISING WHILE STAYS OUT OF THE WAY

CHORUS
YOU'RE THE BEAR - BEST (WHO)
ATTACKS WITH RAGE FROM OUTTA YOUR CAGE
YOU'RE THE BEAR - BEST
MAYESTORS OF THE NFL STAGE

CHICAGO, THAT'S THE HOME OF THE BEARS
AND WHEN YOU WALK DOWN THE STREETS,
EVERYONE STARES
IT'S ALL ABOUT PIGSKIN AT THAT YOU'RE
THE BOMB
EVEN YOUR TEAM
PLAYS IT CALM

$ CHORUS
TO PLATTEVILLE THAT'S WHERE YOU ARE
ALL SUMMER LONG YOU TRAIN, YOU TRAIN, ENDING
WITH A BANG, IT'S FLY PATTERN, PASS, TOUCHDOWN, KICK
WITH THE EXTRA POINT YOU'RE LOOKIN' MIGHTY SLICK

RONI AND NOAH'S WINNING ROUTINE.

WHAT ANNE AND TARA BOUGHT FOR THEMSELVES AND THE CAST

DAN: Tupelow Honey CD
TARA: Hair—color and cut
NOAH: Hair—green dye and cut
ANNE: Haircut and Gap overalls
RONI: Manicure
JON: Pencils and a cassette

TARA

TARA: On <u>Road Rules</u>, they always show girls bitching and fighting. Watch our episodes, and you'll see that barely happens at all. Especially with me and Anne. We were best friends, we were always there for each other. I wish they made as big a deal about that as they did about me and Dan.

TARA'S IDEAL <u>ROAD RULES</u> CAST:

KIT from Season One, TIMMY and CHRISTIAN from Season Two, VINCE from Season Four, and ME and ANNE from Season Five.

WHAT'S TARA GOING TO BE WHEN SHE GROWS UP?

JON: A hand model
NOAH: Anything that allows her to compete
RONI: Working at MTV
ANNE: Tara will be working with kids. She's amazing with kids.
DAN: She'll start her own dating service.

It was a huge part of the trip for me, my friendship with Anne.

Viewers should remember that they edit these shows to death. And they should also remember that you can't always look your best—especially when you're shoveling horse manure. And, hey, not everyone is proud of how they act all the time.

JON: I learned a lot about myself from Tara. She was the hardest on me, but in the end, I really appreciated it.

I just had my clothes stolen... I don't care I'll just borrow ☺

This is m Light ♥

LIMBO!!!

I million Dollars!!

ANNE: I think of Tara as my little sister, my best friend, and my baby chicken. She's so versatile, so multifaceted. She's a tomboy, a tough girl, but she's so sensitive. There are so many different sides of her, and they're all amazing.

NOAH: I'd say that for 80 percent of the trip, Tara was rude to me. I think it's great that she's intelligent and opinionated, but I don't think it's great that she's unwilling to see other people's viewpoints. Tara thinks that L.A. is the center of the universe.

Tara

Have you ever seen the movie Savannah smiles?

DAN: Sometimes I disappointed Tara by not being more present, by not giving her everything she needed. But, despite that, we were really, really close. I hate the thought of not being with her every day.

RONI: Tara's great, she's great. But she holds a grudge for too long. She doesn't realize that people look to her on how to act and that sometimes she can be a source of negative energy.

DESIGNED BY ROAD RULES CAST

JON'S JOURNAL

MISSION

Baby-sit three little piglets for a week! Take them to Noah's, accompany them to a hotel, then deposit them on a farm. Have a squealin' good time!

Day 38
Pigs in Chicago

Hi!

Talking to Tara is like running through a mine field. She's got low self-esteem, but at the same time, thinks she's hot stuff. Case in point, because she's having more fun than I am on this trip, she feels like she's superior to me. So, with this feeling of power driving her, she reaches out a helping hand to pull me up. We talk about things, why I'm having a bad time, and what they can do to change. All well and good, no big deal. But then Tara reaches her hand out a bit too far, flexing a little too much muscle. She says "Tell me what I do that you don't like." Now here is where it gets complicated. Tara is fragile. If I tell her, she'll break. But if I make her feel fragile by being easy on her, she'll know I think she's fragile, which will also make her break. So what I have to do is not burst her bubble, let her keep feeling superior, while not crushing her. I have to humor someone humoring me. So, I tell her the least significant, obvious thing she does that I don't like. And she still gets defensive and somewhat insulted. If I told her I think the way she uses drinking as a social crutch, joins groups to sacrifice her individuality for the power of numbers and acceptance, and dates guys who make her feel cool and strong only to break up with them once the relationship becomes too much work or too deep, she would be crushed beyond repair. We wouldn't be friends anymore, and she wouldn't feel good about herself. The only things Tara does that I don't like are because she has low self-esteem. I think the same thing about Noah. The only reason he's so bossy and show-offish is because he has to prove something to himself. He doesn't think he's good enough. Same goes for getting girls. If he didn't have low self-esteem

Talking to Tara Is Like Running Through a Mine Field

he wouldn't have to over achieve in every aspect of his life.

The reason I think I'm not having as much fun as the others is my life ruled before I got here. From the sound of it, their lives didn't. Even Dan's life couldn't compare to mine. Great school where I can take any class I want, friends that are closer than most families, a mother and a brother who support me emotionally in everything I do, who make me feel like I'm the greatest thing in the world. I've got a truly deep and loving relationship with a girl, two girls actually. I can screw around with one of them, but screwing around isn't important to me — it doesn't constitute a relationship. But anyway....

To me its a great sign of character how people deal with the pigs. Tara and Anne are very good people, and they treat the pigs well. Dan is apathetic, a neutral guy. Noah and Roni are insensitive to the pigs. I'm getting pissed. I still don't get Dan. I can't figure out where the line between who he is and who he thinks he should be is. I think his personal rule of "Always be the best" over-rules the "Be Nice" rule. I blame it on sports. Sports teach kids a lot of stupid stuff: that superiority and esteem come from winnings that there are absolute rules to how everyone should act and be; that its o.k. to lose your individuality to the group. Oh yeah, I forgot one: Its great to be cocky. These rules happen to coincide with all of Dan's flaws. Coincidence? I think not.

I guess my feelings are mixed about all these people. I think overall, I like being with Dan the most. He's just damn likable. But Anne is also super cool and probably we share the most in common. Tara is extremely interesting, funny and smart in my kinda way. Noah, deep in his heart is the most like me. Immaturity is just blocking that right now. Seeing him with his family showed me that. And Roni is fun to be with because we are polar opposites. I never expect her to say what she says or do what she does. I could never be bored around her. I really do love that girl.

I just want to be home. I kick myself for it, but I can't not think that. I love my home and everything about it. But I love this too. I wouldn't want to leave. There is no cure. I can't be happy all the time, and I'm cool with that. I just wish everyone else were.

Jon

RONI TALKS BACK!

RONI: Watching the shows about the pigs made me mad. It looks like I didn't take care of the pigs at all. That's so not true! I was tending to those pigs the whole time! I was cleaning them and everything. And they were three little pains in the asses, believe me. They'd bite at your ankles.

ROAD RULES V: THE LOST EPISODES

and MORE

PIGS

PIGS

PIGS

RONI: Here's a mission that got cut out of the show. When we returned the three little pigs, the farmers told us we had "one more delivery to make." It turns out a mama pig was going to give birth, and we had to deliver the piglets. We had to check on the mama pig in half-hour shifts.

ANNE: It was my turn to check on the mama pig. Out of the goodness of her heart, Tara came with me. We hit the pig pen, and, oh my gosh, there was a little piglet running around. What did Tara do? She screamed "Oh my God!" and ran out. She just left me there. So, I just went around the back of the mama pig and pulled on the little baby piglet and directed him to the milk. Little baby piglets are shriveled-up little messes of goop, but they're such little cute shriveled-up messes of goop. You can't help but love them.

RONI: At one point, the mother pig rolled over on top of her little infants and just wasn't getting up. They were squealing and everything, but she just wouldn't get up. So I hit her in the butt and got her up. She was a little mad, but she was suffocating her own babies. The miracle of life is an amazing thing.

WHAT THE CAST NAMED THEIR BABY PIGS

ANNE: Isaak—for Chris Isaak. Emily, after a friend.

DAN: Jay, for my friend at home. Jane, because it was the plainest name ever.

RONI: Malcom, for Malcom X. Martin, for the sound guy.

TARA: Jack, for Jack Kerouac. Noelle, for my best friend.

JON: Marcus and Meatball.

NOAH: None

Dan: Before the pigs came, we were on milking duty.

WHO DID WHAT WINNIE DAMAGE?

TARA: I crashed into a hotel, scraping the side of the Winnie and breaking a window and a porch light.

JON: I ran the Winnie into the side of a gas pump.

NOAH: I busted the hub caps.

RONI: None of the damage was mine.

ANNE: I wore out the carpet with my crutches.

DAN: None that I remember.

GETTING PERSONAL

DAN: Tara found this newspaper with personal ads in the back, and she was cracking me up, reading them to me aloud. I was driving the Winnie, and she was sitting in the front seat. I was trying to figure out where we were going, but Tara didn't care. All she wanted to do was read these ads. She just loved them.

Tara Writes Her Own Personal Ads

Jon: SM, 21, ISO SF—age, race, religion don't matter. I'm looking for first a friend, then more. I'm fun, a little zany, someone you can really talk to. Ladies, you'll find your best friend in me. Please call!!

Roni: SBF, 19, professional dancer with a great outlook seeks SBM, 19-25, who has a solid body to go with a solid mind. ISO a good time, we will talk, go dancing, must make me laugh!!! N/smokers, don't need to drink to have fun.

Dan: I am the apple-pie-eating, baseball-playing boy of your parents' dreams! SWM, 21, future rock star seeks SWF to goof around with and really talk to. I can make you laugh. My friends call me Danocek, but you can call me Muffin!

Noah: Ladies, you feelin' lucky? SJM, early 20s, seeks beautiful, special woman to share my time and affection w/. Me: into my music, very sensitive, former MTV star. You: sexy, sweet, maybe with a little attitude. We: will make sparks fly. Call!

Roni gives one to Anne!

Anne: A 16-year-old in a 23-year-old's body. This Nancy Kerrigan look-alike is searching for a fun-loving, intelligent guy who will not rush her into marriage but is willing to hang in there and nurse her back to health every now and then.

And Anne Gives One to Tara!

Tara: Have you been featured in Surfer magazine? Do you braid a good braid? Do you know all the words to every Sublime song? Can you recognize great hair when you see it? Sweet, sensitive, native Californian who would be willing to give a piggy-back ride for miles if you sprain your ankle seeks a guy who thinks L.A. is the center of the universe, makes great coffee, is willing to share tube socks and carry my ID and money for me. If interested, send me a pic and scrawl your name and phone number on the inside cover of the book On the Road by Jack Kerouac.

EIGHT THINGS ANNE WANTS YOU TO KNOW ABOUT ROAD RULES V

1. Roni slept in a sleeping bag zipped up to her face like a cocoon.
2. Jon used Elmo soap.
3. Dan's feet are always baby soft.
4. Tara is obsessed with rainbows.
5. Jon wanted a nickname. He wanted everyone to call him "Fats."
6. We pay-per-viewed Liar, Liar and Austin Powers in hotels.
7. We didn't have an instruction manual for the Winnie and had to ask people in trailer parks: "Umm, do you know how we dump our you know what'?"
8. Dan stuck wads of gum onto the Winnie to save for later.

NOAH

NOAH: <u>Road Rules</u> was a 100 percent different from what I had expected it to be. I made friends, but maybe not necessarily the kinds of friendships I'd expected to make. Don't get me wrong, I had a lot of great times; we all did. It's just difficult to be with people who see the world in such completely different ways.

The trip made me realize that I'm not always as right as I think I am. Sometimes I alienated myself from the group. I know that I was wrong a lot of the time, that I

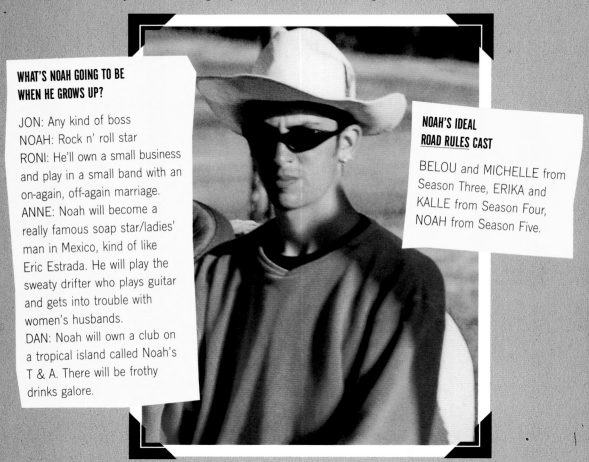

WHAT'S NOAH GOING TO BE WHEN HE GROWS UP?

JON: Any kind of boss
NOAH: Rock n' roll star
RONI: He'll own a small business and play in a small band with an on-again, off-again marriage.
ANNE: Noah will become a really famous soap star/ladies' man in Mexico, kind of like Eric Estrada. He will play the sweaty drifter who plays guitar and gets into trouble with women's husbands.
DAN: Noah will own a club on a tropical island called Noah's T & A. There will be frothy drinks galore.

NOAH'S IDEAL ROAD RULES CAST

BELOU and MICHELLE from Season Three, ERIKA and KALLE from Season Four, NOAH from Season Five.

instigated fights, that I acted like the victim in certain situations when maybe I wasn't. So I guess you could say I learned a lot. I inherited a lot of self-doubt. I'm still young, so I think that's good. I'd rather work through these things now.

I hate gossip. I hate gossip. So watching the show on television can be kind of crazy. That's what a lot of the episodes are like—gossipy. I try not to take them too seriously. My friends sit around drinking and watching the show. They call me after it's over and make fun of me. Some things are embarrassing, but I think that overall I came off okay. As for my family, they love it, but my brother keeps waiting for them to show the real Noah.

ANNE: I adore Noah, but he can be the most critical person on earth. He can never straight-out compliment you. If he tells you that you look beautiful, two seconds later he has to tell you that you look ugly. It's like he's always retracting the good. He doesn't want to feel like he's giving too much or leaving himself vulnerable.

JON: In the beginning of the trip, I thought Noah was a clown. He didn't seem to respect anyone and bossed everyone around. But I think he changed a lot. By the end, I felt close to him and sympathetic to him. I tried to be in his corner as much as possible. I think he needed me there.

TARA: Noah enjoys conflict. He says things just to piss people off. At least that's how he was in group situations. One on one, he was different. He'd actually listen to you and try to understand you. No jerky comments. I liked talking to him a lot—but only in one-on-one situations.

RONI: Noah and I bonded, because we both had art forms that we cared about. He had guitar, and I had dance. It brought us closer together, knowing that we both had these creative forces empowering us.

DESIGNED BY ROAD RULES CAST

DAN: Noah is a really good arguer, and that scared me. It kept me from telling him how I felt sometimes. I regret that we weren't closer, and partially that's my fault: I didn't lay it on the line with him.

CALLING ALL DOCTORS! STAT!

Emergency! Become doctors for a day (plus some!). Stay awake. Stay alert. And try not to pass out! (That means you, Noah!)

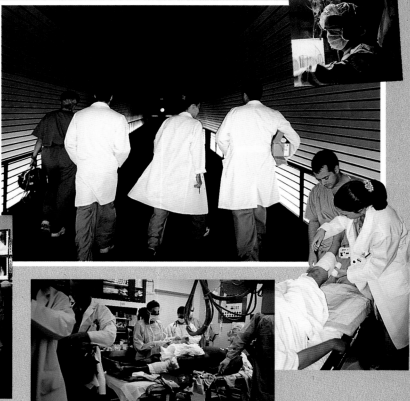

ANNE: The ER was crazy. Tara had food poisoning. Noah was passing out. It was just nuts. And we didn't really get to sleep, because we went to a party afterward. Of course, I was up for it. I knew that Tim would be there.

Party at Lisas. ——> Tim was there didnt come up and talk to me and didnt page me - I thought he didnt like me but finally when I was alone he came up we talked and decided to go to a bar by ourselves - went to 5th Ave. good bar, great band Twistin. Tarantulas. had an amazing time - kissed on camera great - I'll just die if that airs its like PDA in its most extreme form.
8/11 spent the night at Tims we made out. nothing too big happened but still. I stayed there - big step for me. He had to

ANNE'S DIARY

52

℞ from the prescription pad of...DR. TIM

Having cameras all around me was really weird at first. At work being so busy made it easier. But when I was off work, and just hanging out—then I really felt the cameras presence. At that party we had, I was completely freaked-out. I knew the camera guys wanted me to kiss Anne in front of them. It was really crazy.

By the time I went to visit Anne in Toronto, I'd forgotten the cameras were there. Maybe because I was so tired, I'm not sure. Between working and partying with the Road Rules kids, I was getting an average of two hours of sleep a night. It was killing me.

I enjoyed Anne. Anne was interesting. When she was with me, she was so relaxed. She used to page me in the middle of the night. I really liked that too. It made me feel really good.

As far as their visit to our emergency room goes, Anne was really the most into it. She was the only cast member who stayed up all night. It was a very crazy, busy night there. I don't think a third of it got on camera. Anne was really into caring for the patients. It was very touching.

Of course, I loved all the kids. Roni, especially. Jon was whacked, great but whacked. I still speak to Tara about once a month. She and Dan called me together once. That was really great. Noah, well, he was obviously very into Anne. He tried to be buddy-buddy with me, but it was kind of like he was trying too hard. Funny thing is he ended up getting together with a friend of mine who they all called "Dr. Debbie."

Everyone in the hospital watched the episode together. I was teased to heck. They're all calling me "Dr.Tim" now. That's what she called me.

ANNE: In Detroit, Jon wanted to be Tim's best friend, and it became a problem. Tim and I were getting closer and closer. We were really liking each other, and we were running out of time together. As much as I wanted to hang out with everyone on the trip, I wanted some alone time. So one o'clock rolls around, and Tim's like, you know, "Let's go to bed." And Jon says, "Can I sleep over?" Everyone else is going home, and he's going to sleep over? He ended up staying on the computer until four A.M. It was really weird. Then when Tim came to visit me in Toronto, Jon did it again. He stayed up with us in the Winnie all night. It was crazy.

RUNNING

INTERFERENCE

PART DEUX

NOAH: Yeah, it's true, I kissed Dr. Debbie. I had to stand behind a tree to keep her away from the cameras.

back to the winnie I was kind of excited to mess around be w/ him alone but noooo... Jon had to "run interfere — Jon had to "talk" to us forever I fell asleep on Tim listening to Jon We woke up fully clothed no covers still wearing our party clothes Damn. Night #2 ruined.

We got

ANNE'S DIARY

THE LOST EPISODES OF <u>ROAD RULES V</u>

HAIRSPRAY

Toronto
Brampton
• Halton
• Milton   • Nississauga
           • Oakville

RONI: You don't see it in the show, but we had this whole other mission in Toronto. We had to style one another's hair. Noah got happy with the hair spray on Tara's head, and she was not enjoying it. He just let loose. I did Anne's hair up all big and slick, and she looked pretty good. I'm pretty proud of it.

JON: Noah did the worst thing a guy can do to me. He thickly gelled all my hair down and put one little curl out and spray-painted it black. It looked horrendous. I don't know why the others liked it.

TARA: I was about ready to kill Noah. He put my hair in a beehive, which basically meant putting 4,000 tangles in and then cementing it with bobby pins and hair spray. Basically, he ripped my hair out. And then Jon's sitting next to me, muttering under his breath, "Oh, ouch, that's so mean." That is such a Jon thing to do. He can be so frustrating. When you're in a bad mood, he can always make it worse. Not to mention the fact that his hair looked good. I mean, I hate the curl in the middle of his forehead, but basically it looked good.

JON AND JEN

JON: In Toronto, my girlfriend, Jen, came up to visit. I was really happy to see her. We kind of have the relationship that old people have after they've been married for a long time. They really like each other, but it's not so hormonal. I was more relieved than excited that she was visiting. Having her with me made me feel more relaxed and more like myself than I had for a while. Which is a good thing.

ANNE: Jon and Jen have this weird relationship. We were all kind of obsessed with it. He didn't even tell us she was coming. It was like she just kind of showed up in our room. From the moment they saw each other, they were about two inches away from each other, just face to face talking to each other in these real low voices. They were very lovey, lovey, kissy, kissy, and she was kind of like a little puppy dog following him around. It was nice to see him relaxed, because he'd seemed pretty angry for awhile.

JON: This is my rendition of me feeling really frustrated and bottling it up because I didn't want to take it out on someone who didn't deserve it.

DAN

DAN: I love watching the shows. I see one clip, and all of a sudden, there are all these memories. Usually I watch them by myself. Sometimes Anne or Tara will call, and it's just like I have to hang up on them. I need to concentrate.

WHAT'S DAN GOING TO BE WHEN HE GROWS UP?

ANNE: A folk singer
TARA: A rock star or a business man
NOAH: A triathlete
JON: A comedy writer
RON: Living in a big house, behind a white picket fence

DAN'S IDEAL ROAD RULES CAST:

KIT from Season One, TIMMY and CHRISTIAN from Season Two, CHRISTINA and SUSIE from Season Six.

DAN: Okay, we were completely sober when we took this. We were feeling a little scandalous, that's all. We decided to heat things up a little bit. No, there was no sexual tension between Anne and me.

THE DEFINITION OF "PORN"

There's this word I use all the time: "porn." I don't mean it in the traditional sense. I use it as an adjective, like: "That's so porn." When something is porn, it's kind of over-the-top, like really funny yet really bold. Like a guy who's wearing white high tops with skin-tight black acid wash and a tie-dyed top, that's porn. It's cheesy, but he thinks he looks great. When I shaved an "S" for my last name in my chest hair...that was porn.

My goal was to have everyone saying "porn" by the end of the trip. Even the crew was saying it.

ANNE: I love that Dan is a feelings guy. He can talk about how he feels and how he thinks others feel. It's a really unique thing where guys are concerned. He's always trying to pull things out.

JON: Dan is so capable, so intelligent, so charming, so good-looking. But I think he feels like people expect him to be all those things, and therefore he can't let them down. He feels he has a lot to live up to.

TARA: What's there to say? Dan's just wonderful. He's so open and so loving. At the end of the trip he gave me a ring he got from a vending machine. He gave it to me because he thought I'd sketch out at such a couple-y thing to do. But I liked the ring, and I showed it to everyone. We were joking around, saying it was a promise ring.

RONI: Dan handles being the best at everything pretty well. But there's a lot of pressure on him to be the best. I think it must be hard for him, but he's able to handle it.

NOAH: Dan is Mr. No Conflict Guy, but when you actually get to talking to him, it turns out he has a lot of opinions. I think he withheld a lot of what he was feeling toward the group.

DESIGNED BY ROAD RULES CAST

ROAD RULES A-GO-GO

MISSION

Boogie down, Road Rulers! Get on the go-go box, and shake your groove thang!

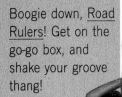
A CARD FROM JON

NOAH A-GO-GO!
NOAH: I like pretty girls, okay? What's wrong with that?

DAN: I like Noah, but if I had a sister I wouldn't let her near him. He's not only disrespectful of girls, he's manipulative with them. The whole Toronto mess with Natascha was just blatant and stupid. He's a smart guy. He knows what he's doing. He should find a better way to deal with his need for affection.

For Roni,

to a bizillion people — I finaley decided to wear a silver skirt and a black shirt that said PRRR... across it

ok that looks nothing like me but general idea.

black
silver

ANNE'S DIARY

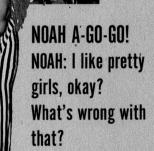
Joker

58

honest — Roni, Tara and I
sat around trying to figure
out how many people Noah
has "been" with:
1) Sandy — Seattle 6) 2 immigration
2) Sari — Calgary   agents
3) other RA — Madison 7) Larisa
4) Laura — Minn.   8) Natasha
5) Debbie — Detroit

I can't believe its been that
many and the funny thing
is is that it would have been
more if girls were willing. We

Toronto

Toronto is the place that I think of when I want good memories of the group. It was the only city where all six of us really got along. We had a lot of fun partying and dancing and drinking and we almost never fought. I remember word for word what Tara said at the Phoenix — "Noah, I love you you're the best person to go out with" That really meant a lot to me. And for a very short-lived moment I felt as if Tara and I could be friends. But that passed, as did getting along with the group.

While I still think back to Toronto as the place where we all were friends, I also think of Toronto as the place I began to f**k up. Between all the girls at clubs and Larissa and Natascha, I pretty much almost ruined my relationship with Rebecca. It took me weeks to convince Rebecca I'd never cheat again and although she got back together with me she still can't trust me 100%. I don't blame her... I not only cheated on her, but I cheated on

I don't know what the f**k thing. Maybe it was the length that I hadn't slept with anyone, but that was it. I really think ching out to anyone else (again for someone to talk to to party with, and then things just got out of control. I started doing what I used to do in high school and on vacations — hooking-up for the sake of hooking-up. And at one of my weakest and loneliest moments of the summer I actually thought I fell in love with Natascha. She was beautiful, intelligent, sweet, funny, exotic... everything anyone would ever want in a girl. But she wasn't Rebecca. It just took me too long to figure that out and everyone involved ended up getting hurt. What's new? I always end up hurting girls, no matter what.

NOAH'S TOP FOUR
ROAD RULES REGRETS

#1. I should have either remained faithful to Rebecca or broken up with her. I like meeting new people. I'm a lot better at meeting nice-looking girls than anything else. It's a bad habit. I really wish I hadn't hurt Rebecca like I did.

#2. I wish I'd been a lot easier to live with. I wish I'd cared less about being places on time and gotten less uptight. I should have chilled.

#3. Dan and I were on the road to being good friends, and then when he started going out with Tara—who never liked me—he stopped hanging with me. At the end of the trip, we both agreed we should have been friends.

#4. Right from the start, I connected with Roni. I should have spent more time with her. Also, I wish I'd not gotten so annoyed at Anne and Tara and the way that they are.

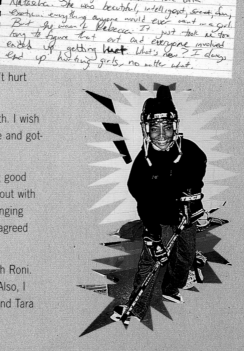

NOAH: I don't think Anne was jealous of my meeting girls. But I do think she was jealous of the fact that I got really into that one girl, Natascha. I don't think she liked that the connection was an emotional one and not just a physical one.

MISSION

They shoot, they score! (Well, maybe not.) Road Rulers, take the rink. And remember, ice hockey's no kiddy sport!

RONI: The Rink Rats were the rudest kids I have ever met. They were just terrible. I had this trick to keep them in line. I learned it from karate. You hit them in the solar plexus, and it just knocks the wind out of them. Only for a second, but it works.

Keep the memories alive!
Make your own

ROAD RULES
SCRAPBOOK!

RONI AND NOAH VS. THE THREE MUSKETEERS

RONI: At the end of the trip, Dan, Tara, and Anne just became this clique. It was like they were one person. I think it was basically because of Tara. She was hanging with Anne, and Dan was following her around. So it was just the three of them. Noah didn't take that well. It was getting on his last nerve. For me, it didn't matter much. The whole trip, I didn't have anyone to really turn to. I sort of went off on my own the whole trip.

When we were in New York City, the group didn't take any interest in my life, in my friends, in my dance company. Noah came and met my dance company, but the rest of them didn't. It was a big awakening for me. I assumed they were better people. In many ways, I wish the fight had happened earlier—that way, I could have gotten over it and moved on.

NOAH: Dan and I used to hang out, but then he and Tara got joined at the hip and I was pushed out. When Anne joined them, it was just, like, forget it. There was no room for me anymore.

The day I spent meeting Roni's friends was one of the best days of the trip. Anne, Dan, and Tara really missed out. I know they feel bad, but I think if we went back in time, the same thing would happen all over again.

Talking w/ Noah turned out really well. I wasn't fair in how I approached him— coming in totally crying & waking him up. But we got everything off our chests, & I really like him, I always have. Now I feel like we can get along.

It makes me feel so bad to know that our '3 Musketeers' makes others feel left out. It never occurred to me anyone would want to be thrown in the crack. D. & I have always said we wanted our relationship to add to, not take away from our experience on this trip. Doesn't look like we've succeeded. Am I just an incredibly insensitive person? Obviously I am— 1st Jon, then Roni, now Noah— I've hurt them all & it's all come out w/in a span of 4 days.

N. said, "If you can leave this trip knowing you've felt good about yourself on it, then you're set for life." It makes each of us question ourselves to the very core of how we are & why, & then examine whether or not we are ok w/ ourselves. Right now I don't like myself very much.

"M" STUDS... Prrr...

Tired....

ok.. pretend that we like each other

Dan's lucky we got on our page!!

Tara and B.F.F. Tina

Smokin'

Help my head is swelling!

can you see up my nose?

DAN TALKS BACK!

DAN: I can't stand watching the episode where Roni yells at us. Not because of Roni—she was totally right—but because of Noah. I can't stand how righteous he acts, as if he was this great guy the whole trip. When I saw that episode, I started yelling at the TV I was so mad.

JON

JON: It's hard to imagine that people beyond my town actually watch the show. Then again, I was hanging out at a New York City club with Kalle from Season Four, and people kept coming up to us, asking, "Are you guys from Road Rules?"

JON'S CHRISTMAS LIST

NOAH: Wire sculpture
ANNE: Phillip Michael Thomas record (Tubbs from Miami Vice)
TARA: Hand-drawn picture and a tape of "Savannah Smiles"
RONI: Back massager and the Magic 8 Ball
DAN: Wire sculpture

JON'S IDEAL ROAD RULES CAST

KIT from Season One, TIMMY from Season Two, BELOU from Season Three, VINCE from Season Four, JON from Season Five, and PIGGY from Season Six

JON AND FOOD

JON: I hate mixing ingredients. For example, I can't have any toppings on my pizza. I have to eat all items in a salad separately and one by one. If there's lettuce, I need to eat all the lettuce before I eat the cucumbers.
I hear that there are people who have overstimulated taste buds. I think I'm one of them. I can eat paper and be like, "Mmmmm, tangy."

WHAT'S JON GOING TO BE WHEN HE GROWS UP?

NOAH: The next Jim Henson
RONI: Working with kids and traveling around visiting Road Rulers from different seasons.
ANNE: He will be the cartoon guru. People will come from miles around just to get a glimpse of his cartoons. He will conduct classes on grassy knolls, and when he dies there will be a huge shrine constructed of him in Japan.
DAN: On the Web
TARA: A great artist

I feel like a spectacle at all times. I try to keep in touch with everyone from Road Rules. I sent them all hand-knit socks for Christmas. Is that cheesy? I just wanted them to know how much they mean to me. I also sent them other stuff. Roni got me a virtual pet from Kentucky Fried Chicken. She was the only person who got me something. That's okay.

I got my butt kicked on Road Rules—in all different sorts of ways. It made me a stronger person, emotionally and physically.

TARA: Jon's great, because he's always willing to tell you how he feels about you. He's eccentric, of course, but he's honest.

RONI: You don't see this on the show, but we went white-water rafting. An unfortunate thing happened: Our raft started to flip, and I slid into Jon and apparently hit him upside the head and injured him. I didn't do it on purpose, and I felt bad about it, and I was choking under the water myself. But Jon wanted me to apologize over and over again. He can be kind of dramatic when he's feeling sorry for himself.

NOAH: At first, I thought Jon was an insecure guy. But I think a lot of times he just played that way. Pretending he didn't know what was up was his way of swaying people to get what he wanted. He's really funny and really smart. He knows exactly what he's doing!

ANNE: Jon is an extremely sensitive person. He started out on the trip being very PC and not wanting to hurt anyone or offend anyone. By the end, he was all snippy and abrasive—just like the rest of us! I think we may have created a monster!

DAN: Jon is very sincere. I know that we'll always be friends. Even if we don't talk for a month or two or however long, I know that when we talk again, it'll be cool. We'll have our friendship back in no time.

DESIGNED BY ROAD RULES CAST

THE ROAD RULES GAMES

MISSION

<u>Road Rules V</u> cast, meet your makers! It's a final mission of Olympic proportion!

Real Worlders —

Eric — went to high school with him for like 3 mos — he made waves goodlooking, funny, maybe a little bossy.

Sean — So funny — out of the guys probably my fav. hot domineering flirty — I had so much fun w/ him

Cynthia — That girl is so funny — expresses everything that is on her mind I really liked her. She was my favorite on Miami show — I thought she was even better in person

Jon — Great guy — so nice I felt very comfortable with him right off — he was the first one to ask me how I was

ANNE'S DIARY

JON: I went out to dinner at an Italian place with Jon B., Eric, and Rachel one night, and they were ordering up a storm. They were on a budget, too, so I was kind of wondering what was up. I mean, it was so absurd. Eric told the waiter he would need to order a side portion of the marinara sauce before he could have it on his entrée. I guess he needed to see if it was up to his MTV-royalty status. When it came, he tasted it and was like, "Unacceptable. Take it away, garçon." Ooooh, sorry, Prince Eric.

RONI: I loved those All-Stars girls, but they were all hair and makeup! We were like little Rug Rats in comparison.

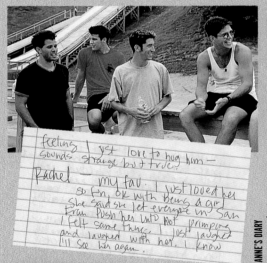

feeling I just love to hug him — sounds strange but true?

Rachel — my fav. I just loved her so fn. ok with being a girl She said she let everyone in San Fran push her into not primping I felt same thing. I just laughed and laughed with her. I know I'll see her again.

ANNE'S DIARY

NOAH AND RACHEL

DAN: In Lake Placid right before the ice-skating contest, Noah and I were getting ready in the men's bathroom and Rachel came in. She and Noah were flirting a little. She kissed him on the cheek, and I said, "Are you kidding me? Let's see a real kiss!" So they did it. It wasn't much. More than a peck, but that's about it.

For Anne: From Jon

Case #003

An MTV Winnebago sits at the Swiss Acres Motor Inn Wednesday morning after vandals took off the front tires of the vehicle and chained them to the right back wheel. The perpetrators, however, left a note with a clue as to where the chain's padlock key was located.

ANNE'S DIARY

the events from PJ because I missed everything
Can I spell at all?
{ kayak SI (single + double)
Luge SP?
Ski Jump
Double skating }

Competing
Kayak Single — Jon against Eric
Double — Roni/Noah against Rachel Cythia
Luge — Jon/Tara against Sean/Jon
Ski Jump — Dan against Eric
Doubles skating Dan/Noah vs Sean/Cynthia

How fun!! Tim sent me flowers yellow Roses!!! He is so sweet he is really the sort of person that I want to spend forever (W)

Roni's inscription inside: "Get well soon, Anne, I hope for only good luck in your body's future. Love, Roni from Road Rules.

Hope your feeling better H.I.T.
Love, Tim
Mountain Valley Floral

RONI'S DIARY

IT'S SO HARD TO SAY GOODBYE TO PEOPLE YOU HAVE LIVED WITH AND LOVED FOR TEN WEEKS. I NEVER WANTED THIS DAY TO COME. I NEVER WANTED TO WATCH EVERY ONE GO BACK TO WHERE THEY CAME FROM. ALTHOUGH WE FOUGHT AND HAD OUR PROBLEMS, IN THE END, WE STOOD IN THE AIRPORT AS ONE.
    IT'S GOING TO BE SO HARD TO WAKE UP AND NOT HAVE FIVE OTHERS GETTING UP WITH ME. IT'S FUNNY TO THINK HOW FAST YOU CAN GET ATTACHED.
    I'M SITTING ON THIS PLAN ON MY WAY HOME IN TEARS, NON-STOP TEARS. I HAVE NO WORDS THAT CAN REALLY EXPLAIN WHAT I'M GOING THROUGH. I FEEL AS THOUGH I'VE BEEN RIPPED AWAY FROM EVERYTHING I KNOW. NOT HAVING A CAMERA IN MY FACE WHILE I'M FEELING DOWN FEELS IS SO FOREIGN.
    I CAN ONLY HOPE THAT WE MAINTAIN OUR FRIENDSHIP FOREVER. THIS WAS THE GREATEST THING TO HAPPEN TO ME EVER!

NOAH'S DIARY

Lake Placid

Once the PreGames got underway, this was a fuckin' great place. The pizza was good and the Real World All-Stars provided a distraction to our problems within the group. Although I got along well with all of the All-Stars, Rachel and I started a special relationship almost the moment we met. It took me about 3 minutes to realize she is the female me. If that makes sense. From the start she flirted, teased, warmed, crushed, and turned me on, and by the end, I knew we'd see each other again.

The games themselves were awesome, challenging, and so much fun — especially the ice-skating! Dan and I were good together. It kind of made me sad that we didn't do more together the whole summer.

MISSION

Celebrate, Road Rulers! It's a revealing final dinner, a handsome reward, and final farewells.

TARA: I didn't want to leave. I knew it would never be the same. I cried my whole final interview. I gave everything to the show, and it's hard to think that maybe Roni, Noah, and Jon are leaving feeling like I didn't give them enough.

NOAH: Leaving the group was really hard, but mainly because I felt like such an outsider. I wish we could have gone home great friends, these six people who could call one another up when they needed to. I know I brought a lot of this feeling on myself. I guess I just wish I could start over—with a clean slate. But I've learned a lot about myself. And it was worth it for that.

WHERE ARE THEY NOW?

THE HANDSOME REWARD—A TRIP TO GREECE FOR TWO! WHO ARE YOU TAKING WITH YOU?

ANNE: I'm taking my mom. After all she did for me, I owe her one.

TARA: I don't know. I'm thinking of taking my sister.

RONI: I'm taking my mom — of course.

DAN: I'm giving the tickets to my parents. Sean from Real World gave me the idea.

NOAH: I'm taking Rebecca. It's the least I can do.

JON: I'm taking my mom. She's awesome.

ANNE : I'm about to graduate from Arizona State University. I study accounting, but I don't necessarily want to be an accountant. I waitress at a steak house to make money. I'm planning to stay in Arizona my whole life.

ANNE AND DR. TIM

ANNE : I went out to visit Tim a couple of months after the show. It was stormy and miserable, and I wasn't feeling very well, but we fell right back into it—talking, hanging out, having a great time. But he's going to be in Detroit for another three years, and, well, I'm going to be in Arizona, so there's no real way we can work it long-distance. We're seeing other people.

TARA : I'm in my senior year at UCLA. I'm majoring in psychology and still hanging out at the sorority. I'm interning at TriStar. I have no idea what I want to do with my life.

DAN AND TARA

TARA: Dan and I broke up on my birthday. It really wasn't that big of a deal. It was really the distance that messed-up our relationship. And, also there are some differences between us. For instance, he's mushy, and I'm not. He kept trying to make me more comfortable with that stuff. He'd call me "Muffin." I just couldn't deal with it. But, we still speak. We're really good friends.

DAN: I'm in my last year at school at the University of Minnesota. I'm a finance major, but I want to move into something more creative. When I graduate, I think I'll live in Minneapolis and try to get a job. As for Rachel, she moved to Arizona, and goes to ASU. We're friends, although she wouldn't talk to me for a week after the episode about her aired. And she's started hanging out with Anne.

NOAH: I'm living in Madison, Wisconsin, and devoting most of my time to my band, The Lotus Band. I play guitar, manage the band, and book all of our gigs. I'm still going out with Rebecca, but it was a long haul for her to forgive me. I can't say that I blame her.

JON: I'm going to school at Tufts University in Massachusetts. I started a rap group called Cold Hard Cash. I'm MC Cold Hard, and my friend is MC Cash. I'm also really into kaijubig monster wrestling. My monster-wrestler name is Electroshock Trooper. I broke up with Jen. I'm still living with my mom, and I want to keep living with my mom. Is that bad?

RONI: I'm working, taking photography and karate classes, and dancing with Awakening Theater Dance Company. I'm still living with my mom in New York City, but I might go to college upstate next year, in which case I'll move into the dorms.

THEME SONG

This is the true story of five <u>Real World</u> has-beens.

Picked to go on an adventure.

To win the handsome reward.

We got Cyn Dog from Miami
and Jon from L.A.
We got Rachel coming down
from the 'Frisco Bay.
We got Eric from New York
and Sean from Bean Town.
We packed up all our gear,
we're on our way now.

<u>Road Rules</u>!

All-Stars!

ROAD RULES ALL STARS

RACHEL

Last Seen:
The Real World
Reunion
First Seen:
The Real World
San Francisco
Lives In:
Los Angeles, California
Birthdate:
October 22, 1971
Occupation:
Teacher/Actress

JON

Last Seen:
The Real World
Reunion
First Seen:
The Real World
Los Angeles
Lives In:
Owensboro, Kentucky
Birthdate:
July 30, 1974
Occupation:
Country Singer

SEAN

Last Seen:
The Real World
Boston
Lives In:
Minneapolis, Minnesota
Birthdate:
October 3, 1971
Occupation:
Second-Year Student at
Law School

ERIC

Last Seen:
The Real World
Reunion
First Seen:
The Real World
New York
Lives In:
West Allenhurst,
New Jersey
Birthdate:
May 23, 1971
Occupation:
Actor, Entertainer, Music
Producer

CYNTHIA

Last Seen:
The Real World
Miami
Lives In:
Oakland, California
Birthdate:
October 26, 1973
Occupation:
Travel Agent/
Events Planner

WOULDN'T HAVE GONE IF:
That Flora chick was going to be there.

CYNTHIA ON RACHEL'S BEING CAST

CYNTHIA: My first impression of Rachel was "nice shoes". She has a style like my own. She's very petite, like I am. Actually, she's much shorter. Together, she and I weigh about 206 pounds. She's a tiny tot, just like me. She's a very beautiful girl.

She really opened up immediately about the accident she'd been in. I admire her for being able to come out here and physically try to do these things. I think it was really courageous.

RACHEL: I was finishing up my last semester of graduate school at the University of California, San Diego, when they called me to do All-Stars. Just like with The Real World, it was perfect timing. When they wouldn't tell me with whom I'd be going on the road, well, of course I was a little suspicious. But I knew it wouldn't be difficult for me to figure out who was going. I know everybody from The Real World. Everybody.

I figured they'd pick Jon from the L.A. cast. I speak to Beth S. from that cast, and I knew she wasn't invited. And, of course, I knew Tami would never do it. So I narrowed it down to Jon. When I called him, he already knew I was going. He's the one who told me Eric was on the trip. So, three down. Mike from the Miami cast and I have friends in common, so I called him. He told me about Cynthia. One to go. I figured there'd be someone from London, and I was really hoping it'd be Lars. We're really good friends. But he told me he hadn't gotten a call.

Then, a few weeks later, I was at a birthday party at Jacinda's (London cast) house. I ran into Syrus from the Boston cast. He told me that he wasn't going on All-Stars, but he was pissed because his friend Sean was. I was kinda bummed. I thought Syrus was cool, and from what I'd seen of the rest of that cast, probably the coolest of them all.

JON: Eric was really forward about why he was doing <u>All-Stars</u>, and I was cool with that. Actually, I identified with it. Frankly, that's part of my reasoning, too. I want the exposure, too.

Eric was host of <u>The Grind</u>, and he's probably the most famous of all us <u>Real Worlders</u>. I would actually think he'd have more of an attitude than he does. He really stuck up for me at the reunion—at that point, we barely knew each other.

Of course, it didn't make me feel too great when one of the first things he said to me was that he got a record deal. I've been trying to get a record deal for four or five years now. I sing pretty darn good, and I can't get one. I was furious when I heard that. I thought it was very ironic.

ERIC: The main reason I got involved in <u>Road Rules All-Stars</u> was business. There were a lot of things in my career that I was trying to move forward, and I wanted to do a lot of publicity. And as we all know, MTV gives you a lot of exposure all around the world. And that's what I wanted to do—to take my business and the things I'm doing to an international level.

My experience with my <u>Real World</u> roommates was not very pleasant after it ended. I can't explain why my roommates' attitudes changed after I was on <u>The Grind</u>, but they did. I didn't want to put myself in a situation like that again. These shows can be about drama, and I didn't want that. That's why I kept my career as my focus. And, of course, I wanted to have a great adventure.

Before the show started, I hadn't seen a full episode of <u>Road Rules</u>, but from what I'd heard, the experience was about having an open mind. That's why I didn't want to know who was going on the trip with me. I wanted it to be a surprise.

...DN'T HAVE GONE IF:
...dn't let anyone ruin my trip.

CYNTHIA: After <u>The Real World</u>, I stayed in Miami for a few months; then I moved to Atlanta; then I moved back to Oakland. That's where I was ...en they called me for <u>All-Stars</u>.

I was cleaning the apartment when I got the call. ..e first thing I wanted to know was what kind of ...ople I'd be stuck with. After Miami, with all those ...ople groping and being upset all the time, I wanted ... know what to expect. Of course, they wouldn't tell ... I thought they were going to put Puck on the ...ad with us. Just to stick it to us real bad.

I'm really not sure why they picked me. For this ... for <u>The Real World</u>. I really don't know. I mean, why ...n't they pick Sarah for this? She's the athletic ...e. She and I talked about it, and she thought the ...oducers had probably wanted to pair me up with ...chel, because we're such prisses.

I spent the months before the trip preparing ...self mentally. I knew it was going to be very ...ing, but I was still crazy enough to do it. I was excited for the travel-...

..'ve never had the finances to go places, and I knew this was my

SEAN ON CYNTHIA'S BEING CAST

SEAN: I had my first exper...
ence with an African-Ame...
woman on <u>The Real Worl...</u>
<u>Boston</u>. That was Kameel...
Let's just say it wasn't ve...
good. Kameelah had a lo...
racial issues. She also ha...
lot of problems with white...
men. She really just didn'...
like me. I'm from Wiscons...
I haven't had a lot of expe...
ences with black people, ...
I'm just totally top-forty.

So I was pretty scared ...
when I saw Cynthia. I was ...
thinking: "Oh God, is it g...
to be Kameelah all over ...
again?" But right off the b...
Cynthia was nothing like ...
Kameelah. Cynthia was su...
cool. She was nice, friend...
and had a lot of life.

Casting CYNTHIA

WOULDN'T HAVE GONE IF:
When Mary-Ellis informed me that my travel mates would be a surprise, I told her that was fine—on one condition: NO PUCK.

JON: It was Mary-Ellis who telephoned me about doing <u>All-Stars</u>, and I have to say I was pretty surprised when she asked, "So, Jon, are you available to do a <u>Road Rules</u> special?"

"You know what, I'm wide open," I told her. Just like that. It was weird. I'm a pretty busy guy. I've got my music and I do gigs and speaking engagements all the time, but I didn't even have a doctor's appointment scheduled during the period of time they wanted me. It was like it was fate.

I watch <u>Road Rules</u> all the time. My favorite season is the Islands season, although I have to admit, that cast drives me nuts. I would have loved to do those missions, though. Staying on a deserted island? Getting to meet Gilligan? To me, that's cool.

So, I was excited to do the show—but I did want to know who my travel mates were going to be. <u>The Real World</u>—it's kind of like we've created our own little club. There's this long chain of people and contacts; it's like a fraternity we all belong to. So, all I had to do was pick up the phone. Beth told me she'd heard Rachel was going. I spoke to Rachel, and she told me she thought Cynthia would be going, and that she'd heard rumors about Lars and Neil from London. I called Julie from Season One, and she told me that neither she nor Heather had been picked, so I figured it must be Eric. I hated the Miami season—they had absolutely no morals whatsoever—but I liked Cynthia. So I was glad she was coming along, too.

I think Rachel told me about Sean, but I was still surprised when someone from Boston showed up. I guess I was still expecting someone from London. But they were passed over. Just luck, I guess.

RACHEL ON JON'S BEING CAST

RACHEL: Jon is such a sweetheart. We really bonded at the reunion, and I was really, really glad to know he'd be coming with us. In many ways, we have a lot of things in common. We're both really into our families. Both of us come from religious backgrounds. All in all, it made me really comfortable to know that Jon would be around.

ERIC ON SEAN'S BEING CAST

WOULDN'T HAVE GONE IF:
Puck was going to be there. I couldn't handle that guy in such a small space.

S EAN: Around the time we were finishing up <u>The Real World–Boston</u>, I overheard the crew talking about some special they were going to be shooting. At the wrap party, Mary-Ellis took me aside. She said, "We might have something for you coming up." Then she told me about <u>All-Stars</u>. I told her I'd have to get back to her. It was a big decision for me to make: whether to go on <u>All-Stars</u> or not. I'd had to take a year off of law school to do <u>The Real World</u>, and doing <u>All-Stars</u> would mean I had to take off another semester. I talked to my dad, and he ran it through the family chain. Finally, we all decided it was an opportunity I couldn't pass up.

ERIC: There's a part of me that's a little pissed that they would even ask Sean to be on this show. He's just gotten out of <u>The Real World–Boston</u>, and he doesn't know what it's like to be noticed on the street, to feel like you're famous, to feel like you're a star and have that label. His outlook on the show is totally different from ours. I feel sorry that he has to go through this right now. The four of us have been doing this for years. He has no idea what this is really all about.

I'm not a huge <u>Real World</u> viewer, but I'd seen a few marathons, and I pretty much knew who everyone was. I was actually hoping that Eric would be going, but I figured he was too big. I'd seen him on <u>The Grind</u> and everything. And I was also hoping for Jon, although anyone from that L.A. cast would have been cool.

Syrus called me after he went to that party of Jacinda's and told me about running into Rachel. I didn't really remember who she was, but Montana—she's a <u>Real World</u> freak—gave me the lowdown. I looked Rachel up on the Internet. I read all about her—about what she'd been doing since her show, about her accident, everything.

Casting SEAN

WILL THEY GET ALONG?

JON: We were on the train. Eric and I were talking about our <u>Real World</u> experiences. We were both apprehensive about the weeks to come. After all, we've all had our unflattering moments. We certainly didn't need anymore. So, when Rachel and Cynthia got on, we decided that this needed to be a fun trip, that's it. We all made a pact: NO FIGHTING.

FROM THE DESK OF **MR. BIG**

All right, listen up you country-twangin', hips-a-grindin', claw-wearin', Republican-delegatin', log-rollin' Real World All-Stars turned Road Rulers.

This is the new voice of Road Rules. Don't touch that dial. There's nothing wrong with your next clue.

Welcome to Road Rules—Puck style! I'm callin' the shots now, you got that?! And I'll be checkin' in on you guys from time to time, so you better follow my clues—and if you can survive the missions, well then...you might just get that handsome reward.

Okay—get your candy asses Winnie and let's move out!

ERIC: I was stoked in every way to hear Puck's voice and to know he was Mr. Big.

MISSION: THE OLYMPICS

We're number two! We're number two!

MISSION: GHOST-BUSTING!

Come on, get with the spirit!

CYNTHIA AND ERIC

RACHEL: In the beginning of the trip, I felt like Eric was flirting with me. But that might have something to do with the fact that I'm a total flirt. I mean, I'll flirt with anybody. I'll even flirt with Jon.

In Connecticut, when we were in the asylum, we played this game of "Truth or Dare." Someone asked me what I was looking for in a guy. I said that personality was everything. Obviously, that's not something that Eric has much of. Then Sean—somewhat pointedly—asked me how important a guy's education was. "Extremely important," I told him, especially to my parents, who are immigrants. Then Sean asked if Eric would meet my parents' criteria. I had to say that of course he wouldn't. That was the end of Eric's and my flirting.

Oh well.

The next night, Eric and Sean came into our room. I made it clear to Sean that he couldn't stay in my bed, but Cynthia let Eric stay in hers. I sleep like a rock, so I didn't hear anything. Later on, Cynthia told me that something had happened. I think she was informing me in a "back off" kind of way. As if that were necessary.

Anyway, it didn't matter. Eric blew her off. Later on in the trip, when we all were fighting with Eric, Cynthia was out to get him, which was fine by me.

JON: Cynthia and Eric totally got together. They kept it a secret for about a week. I don't think it's a stretch to say that after the encounter, Eric didn't treat her how she would have liked. He's got a big ego and thinks he can get whoever he wants at any time—even Rachel. He didn't treat her too well, either. He was shocked that she wouldn't consider hooking up with him. I think that was a big source of tension between them.

CYNTHIA: I did not tell Rachel that Eric and I got together. I don't know why she would say that. Okay, so Eric and I slept in the same bed, but we just slept. He tried to feel on my booty a little bit; yeah, he was feeling on me a little bit; but honestly, I haven't gone that route yet. I have never had sex with a white man, and Eric is hella white to me. Not that I have anything against that. I just haven't done it yet. But I know Eric is attracted to black women. He said so when we were at the asylum.

Believe me, if Eric and I had gotten together, Rachel would not have slept through it. Anybody who would be with me would be going off. He would be enjoying himself. He'd be vocal. And, come to think of it, so would I.

Since the trip ended, Eric is the only person to whom I've spoken. I'd heard there were rumors circulating that we'd had sex, so I asked him, "Did you know we had sex?"

He just laughed. "Is that right?" he wanted to know.

You know what, I'm cool with Eric. I don't know what he told anybody. Maybe he's used to getting whatever he wants when he lays in a bed with someone. But not with me.

I guess you'll have to hook us all up to a lie detector. The person who's lying will get a shock. I promise, it won't be me.

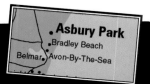

Asbury Park
Bradley Beach
Belmar Avon-By-The-Sea

BOYS vs. GIRLS

ERIC: Cynthia and Rachel, basically if you're on a wilderness adventure, they're not the two best girls to be with. They're definitely a little high maintenance. As an example: We were in Connecticut, and we didn't know where we'd be going next. We didn't know about New Zealand. We thought maybe an island or something. So, there's this slight chance that we might be going swimming, and Rachel goes and gets a bikini wax. I was like, What is this? What kind of show are we on?

The whole trip, Rachel was just in my hair. She was constantly in my face complaining. "Carry this. I need this. I need that." Shut up! Shut up! It just gets overwhelming.

SEAN: I have to say I was totally with Eric on the subject of the girls' complaining—and yes, I mean Rachel too. Rachel is so into her looks. She's an attractive woman. She's naturally pretty. I don't know why she's always powdering herself. It's like, "Get over it! We're on the road!" Like her as much as I do, it made me insane how whiny she was. Come on, girl! Stop pissing and moaning!

JON: Rachel brought one whole bag full of nothing but shoes. She had about seventeen pairs of shoes, I think. And Cynthia, you think she's going to be all smiles, but she's not that way all the time. It's like Dr. Jekyll and Mr. Hyde. If she's hungry and cold, she stops smiling and her fangs just come out. It's like temper-tantrum city, and you better look out!

Those girls were whiners! I have to admit, there were times we wondered: "Now, what would it be like to have an all-guys Road Rules?"

RACHEL: I'm concerned about my physical appearance, I'm not embarrassed about it. I promised myself I'd lose a lot of weight to be on this show. I hated the way I looked on San Francisco. I was fat and too traumatized to exercise. I swore that it wasn't going to happen again. But, of course, I partied the two months before the trip so....

They sent us all these winter clothes. I threw out half of them. I was convinced we were going somewhere tropical.

I was picturing cute little bikinis and shorts, not big bulky sporting gear.

CYNTHIA: My nails are very serious to me. Before I went on the trip, my mother suggested I cut my nails down. I was like, "That is not going to happen." I've never been without long nails, and I'm not going to let three weeks change my whole repertoire. My mother was like, "Well, what if you have to climb a mountain?" I'm like, "Well, I'll just be sticking my fingernails in the mountain, won't I!"

If, God forbid, a nail does break, it'll hurt my feelings, but I'll get over it somehow. My hair, that's a whole other story. I can't run around looking crazy by the head. Before you go on the trip, they tell you that you can have only two bags with you. Well, hell, my hair stuff takes up a whole lot of space! So, in order for me not to have five or six bags, I had to get my hair braided. That way, I didn't have to bring a blow dryer, flat iron, roller set, the whole nine yards. Any black person will know what I was up against. We don't have wash-and-wear hair.

CYNTHIA:
We care how we look? What about Eric? Eric is always naked. He's always taking his shirt off. What I wanted him to do was take his shirt off when we were low on money, let me pimp his ass on the street and get us some damned cash. That would have worked for me.

RACHEL:
Eric's a cute kind of boy, but World War III could be happening and he'd be looking at his pecs.

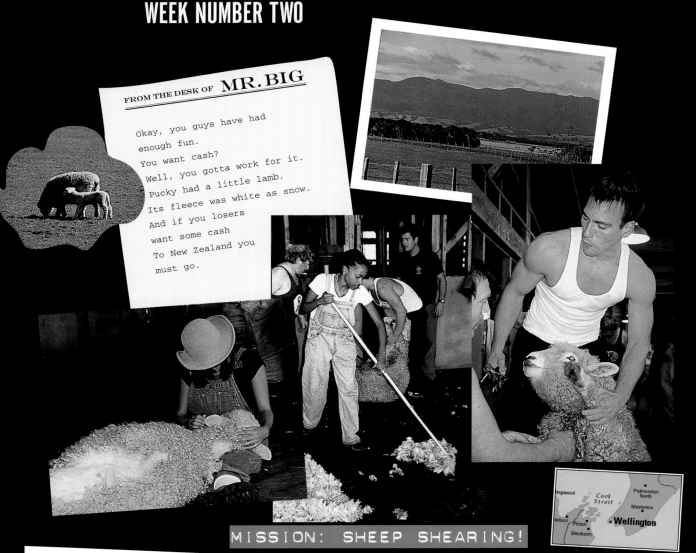

FROM THE DESK OF MR. BIG

Okay, you guys have had
enough fun.
You want cash?
Well, you gotta work for it.
Pucky had a little lamb.
Its fleece was white as snow.
And if you losers
want some cash
To New Zealand you
must go.

MISSION: SHEEP SHEARING!

OUR FIRST NEW ZEALAND MISSION:
It was hard not to cut the sheep when shearing them.

RACHEL:
I'm used to traveling. My
dad was in the military, and
my mom's from Madrid.
I've lived in Turkey and
England. I found being in
New Zealand with these
guys frustrating. All they
wanted to eat was fast
food. I've never eaten so
much fast food in my life!
And when I wanted to buy
the local paper, they got
mad at me for spending
their money!

MISSION: MILK MAIDS!

MISSION: ZORBING!

SEAN: I was so close to barfing in that zorb thing.

MISSION: BLAST OFF!

CYNTHIA: Flying by wire was awesome.

MISSION: RAP JUMPING

We were climbing the walls...literally.

THE LOST EPISODE OF ROAD RULES ALL-STARS

JON: You don't see it on the show, but we tried to make ourselves a little money when we got to New Zealand. It didn't really work.

ERIC: We rolled into Wellington, checked into our hotel, and had no idea where our next money was coming from. So Sean and I went for a walk down through the streets of Wellington. We saw all these different people on the street playing different instruments and stuff. So we were like: "Let's make a couple of extra dollars. We'll take Jon, throw him out there, he'll sing a couple of songs, play his guitar, and who knows? Maybe we'll make some money." We did it. We made about ten dollars. Not bad.

Rachel and Sean

RACHEL: My relationship with Sean changed the night of the fight with Eric in the restaurant. Sean hadn't come to the restaurant, and when we got back to the hotel I told him what Eric had said about not really caring about us. Sean was really hurt. Eric had been telling him they were going to go surfing when they got home, and Sean—he's so small-town—he believed him. I think he was really impressed with all the "Yo, yo, yo" stuff.

Suddenly, I just felt this urge to protect Sean. I wanted to make him feel better. We went out to a bar. The cameras couldn't get into the place, so it was just the two of us. We started playing this game, trying to pick people up. We weren't really interested in the other people; we liked each other. But I don't think either of us was willing to admit it.

From that point on, we were flirting, flirting, flirting. We started hanging out by ourselves, having long talks, going to get food together.

One night in Auckland, we were lying in my bed. Cynthia was asleep and Sean started trying to kiss me and touch me and stuff. I wanted to kiss him, but I also had a boyfriend back home. I was really confused. Just when I thought, "Okay, I'm going to do it," there was a knock on the door. It was Jon, and he had a camera crew with him. Sean was so pissed. But he was also pretty stoked—that was the closest to kissing me that he'd gotten. Our first kiss wasn't until the flight back to Los Angeles. We were sitting together under blankets. He was sweet-talking me, and then we just kissed. It was really nice. Being with him made me realize I didn't care about my boyfriend at home. He was really rich and generous, but Sean's so real. It was all about Sean.

SEAN: Right before we went to New Zealand, I started liking Rachel. We would talk about everything she'd been through, how awful things had been for her, and I just was so impressed with how she was dealing with it all. There was one conversation we had—I think it was the night before we got on the plane and we were lying in bed together— and I was like, "That's it. I like her."

That night of the Eric fight, when we went to the bar, I was sure she was really going after other guys. I still think she was! I didn't think she liked me at all. I knew I liked her more than she liked me. And, it's true, I was feeling like a chump about Eric. But Rachel really straightened me out.

Since Rachel had a boyfriend, she wanted to hide our relationship from the cameras. I really didn't care. I liked her and wanted to kiss her, and didn't care who knew or who saw. But, I tried to respect her wishes as much as possible. Of course, it kind of blew up in our faces at the end. The cameras caught us in a hotel room together. I don't think we were wearing much.

I know it seems like an odd match. What Rachel and I want from life is so different. I'm a midwestern boy. I want the whole big family and marriage dream. And she's all about L.A. But regardless of all that, we really, really bonded. She's a great, great girl. I love watching her laugh.

WEEK NUMBER THREE

FROM THE DESK OF **MR. BIG**

Yo! Wanna-bes.
Here's your ticket to Tinseltown.
This is your REAL chance to
REALLY make it, but REALISTICALLY
speaking,
The REALITY of it is—yeah, right.

The White Zone is for the parking of Winnies only.

MISSION: COOKING
Girls, prepare a MEAL for the boys.

CYNTHIA: I felt really sick after I ate those bugs, really sick. I know every-one thinks I went totally ballistic, which is true, I did; but ask my friends and family and they'll tell you they thought I handled myself well. They said if they were me, they would have really turned it out.

I was pissed off. For all production knew, I was allergic to that stuff that went inside my body. I really felt tricked.

I wish I had done more. I wish I had turned the table over. I felt really violated and taken advantage of. I should have done way more than I did.

They did have to stop filming, though. You're not supposed to talk directly to the cameras, but I started screaming directly at them to book me a flight home.

Of course, I didn't end up going home. It was just like, "Let me be mad for a moment. Let me have my time." Everyone's got their limits, and they pushed me way over, way over mine.

MISSION: COOKING BUGS!
Boys, prepare MEAL WORMS for the girls!

STAYING AT BETH S.'

BETH: It was so great to have the All-Stars at my house, but it was crazy to have the cameras back in my life. Here's one thing I know didn't make it on camera. I have a very small house, so sleeping quarters were really tight. I was sleeping in bed with Eric, and all of a sudden we were kissing. There's not a living thing on this planet that would say that Eric is not totally gorgeous. So I couldn't believe I was kissing him. He's a great kisser, a really great kisser! He tried to take it a bit further, but I didn't want to get too X-rated. I was happy with the kissing.

Fry those corn dogs, stir up that lemonade,
and look real slick at "HOT DOG ON A STICK."

RACHEL: I almost stopped liking Sean at "Hot Dog on a Stick." He was just too comfortable in those polyester shorts. Then again, he was pretty grossed out by me. He couldn't figure out why I was so upset. I know it seemed frivolous—like all I cared about was wearing such cheap clothes—but really that wasn't the whole story.

The "Hot Dog on a Stick" mission was just really embarrassing for me. It brought up a lot of issues. I called my mom in the middle of the fiasco, and she just encouraged me in thinking that it was a degrading and humiliating thing to do, selling lemonade on the street. I was raised in a very European way. My mom thinks of theme restaurants as excuses to humiliate employees.

I was really upset, and my mom used the opportunity to turn on me. At the time, I was still considering whether to move to L.A. and pursue acting. She thought that was a terrible idea and tried to dissuade me. "Is this why you want to move to Los Angeles? To sell hot dogs? Is that why you got a double masters?" she asked me.

I put that outfit on, feeling like I was humiliating my parents on television. I felt bad. I knew the boys were hating me. I also knew that Sean was seeing my snob side, which just made me feel worse. I didn't want him to see me like that. Thank God, I had Cynthia there. She was really supportive. I really appreciated that.

Of course, to add insult to injury, they had us all pose for pictures. "C'mon, hot doggers! Let's have another hot-dog hug!" Horrifying.

JON: Rachel was crying about the cheap polyester right in front of the whole staff. They had to stand there and watch her freak out about what they do for a living. I felt terrible.

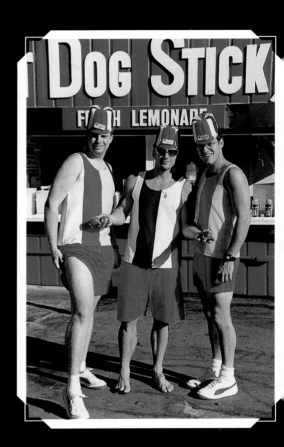

CYNTHIA: For me, the hot-dog mission wasn't that bad. I used to work at a stand at Marine World, so I know how to dip dogs.

I was sittin' up there eating corn dogs and drinking lemonade, when I heard Rachel crying in the bathroom. I asked her what was wrong, and she was like, "My mother's going to kill me. She spent all this money for me to go to school, and she's going to go crazy." I was as nice and as comforting as possible. "Girl, don't trip," I said. "You'll look back at this and crack up. Just put your stupid hat on and don't worry about it." She was hurting. I said, "Now you know how I felt with the bugs." She apologized for not sympathizing with me.

THE END

MISSION: RECORDING STUDIO

RACHEL: We were in this stellar, state-of-the-art recording studio, and Jon was just like a little boy in a candy store.

THE LAST SUPPER

JON: We didn't know our last night was our last night. We thought we still had another day left. So when a limo arrived to take us out to dinner, we were a little surprised.

Eric had warned me that before the show was up, he would tell Rachel everything he thought. The final dinner was his last chance. He kicked me under the table, and I knew what was coming. I was just thinking, "Uh oh."

He just confronted her. "Why are you such a bitch?" They started going back and forth, back and forth. Sean and I were just shaking our heads. It was so sad. I think we were both just sad: "We're going to go out like this?"

When Puck showed up with our handsome rewards, we were so down. It was just anti-climactic. The mood had been spoiled, and we were just bumming. I'm sure we looked really ungrateful.

MISSION: GROUNDLINGS

IMPROVISATION NIGHT Act natural! Be real! You're on!
CYNTHIA: Groundlings—that was my favorite mission.

RACHEL: Eric's criticisms just came out of nowhere. We were sitting around, drinking and looking through pictures. I was trying to make conversation, so I asked the table, "What was your favorite mission?" Eric chirps: "Hot Dog on a Stick—because I saw you suffer." Then he accused me of being ungrateful when he carried my bags. I told him he was the one who was ungrateful, not to mention shallow. It was just awful. Cynthia wasn't feeling well. Jon and Sean were avoiding any confrontation. And I came off like the bitch—as always.

MR. BIG

RACHEL: When Puck showed up, everyone was acting so impressed. Sean was feeling like he just met the biggest celebrity ever. Eric was all over him, wanting to be part of the whole rebel thing. I could not have cared less. I mean, it was nice to see him. He looked good. But big deal.

GOOD-BYE

ERIC: By the time the show was over, I was ready to get back to work. It was nothing personal against anybody. But I was upset with myself. I let myself get caught up in it. But that's what happens when you throw five people together every minute, every hour, every day for three weeks. You can't help but get on one another's nerves. You start to trip out and bum a little bit, and you start to get away from your business, your reality. You get sucked into this vicious circle inside of the show.

JON: I regret that our experience was so tainted by fights—which doesn't mean I wouldn't do it a thousand times over. It's just, I'd try and make it different. As for my cast mates, I don't know. I think Cynthia might have had some regrets about doing the trip. She didn't say good-bye to anyone but me. She just ripped outta there.

CYNTHIA: I was really hoping that Puck would start a scene when he showed up at the final dinner. When he didn't, I wanted him to at least join us for a drink or something. You know, I would have liked to see him do some of his Puck things, like dig into his nose and toss a few boogers around.

Rachel was so molded. If you don't know what that means, it's when you get so embarrassed you turn green. Well, that's how Rachel was. Molded. She blocked herself with her hand, thinking he was going to come and give her some big hug. But he didn't even come near her.

CYNTHIA: All this TV stuff, Cynthia's life does not revolve around that. I had to get going. But you know what? I had a good time. I went through a lot mentally—more than I did on The Real World. But I would do it again. That's how crazy I am!

RACHEL AND SEAN REDUX

SEAN: After the show was over, Rachel and I hung out together in L.A. I still had some time to kill. Second semester of law school hadn't started up yet. I actually lived with Vince (Road Rules Four) for a while. Of course, Rachel wouldn't come visit me. Vince lives in the Valley, and she'd never be caught dead there.

I went back to school, and we stayed monogamous. She comes to visit me here in Minneapolis, and I go back to L.A. often to visit her. She lives with two Real Worlders. Isn't that crazy? She lives with Norm (Real World–New York) and Mike (Real World–Miami). Weird, huh? We've also hung out with Dan from Road Rules (Northern Trail). It's been fun. We're happy together.

My Real World cast members think it's cool, although Montana gives me a hard time about it. She's like, "Oh, so now you guys are like king and queen of The Real World!"

RACHEL: Our little romance really blossomed after the show. We've spent a lot of time together, going back and forth. Sean's and my thing is real. He's just, "What you see is what you get." I love his Midwest thing. It's such a relief to be with someone so kind, with such good values.

I would never have met Sean if it weren't for Road Rules. I would never have gotten to know him at all. So, thank God, I went. I'm head over heels in love with Sean. Did I also say I think he's a total babe?

ROAD RULES VI

Birthdate: 6-15-76
Hometown: Los Angeles, California
Sign: CANCER
Seen Snacking On: Australian corn chips
Heard Listening To: The Pixies
Heard Saying:
"I just wanna be Frisbee free!"

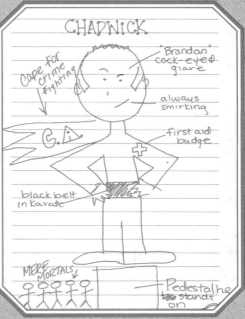

CHADWICK

Birthdate: 9-25-73
Hometown:
Steamboat Springs, Colorado
Sign: LIBRA
Seen Snacking On: Anything healthy!!!
Heard Listening to: The Rent soundtrack
Heard Saying: "I can do that."

KEFLA

Birthdate: 9-10-74
Hometown: Foley, Alabama
Sign: VIRGO
Seen Snacking On: Oranges and bananas
Heard Listening To: Busta Rhymes
Heard Saying: "My bad."

PORTRAIT GALLERY
by Susie

SHAYNE

Birthdate: 12-8-75
Hometown: Sherwood Park,
Alberta, Canada
Sign: SAGITTARIUS
Seen Snacking On:
A McFeast Deluxe
Heard Listening To:
Ben Folds Five
Heard Saying: "Aboot"

PIGGY

Birthdate: 10-27-73
Sign: SCORPIO
Hometown: Middlesborough,
Cleveland, England
Seen Snacking On: Bacon sandwiches
Heard Listening To: George Michael
Heard Saying: "Bollocks!"

SUSIE

Birthdate: 8-10-79
Hometown: Pittsburgh, Pennsylvania
Sign: LEO
Seen Snacking On: Popsicles
Heard Listening To:
Billy JoelHeard Saying:
"That's rad."

WHAT IS YOUR ETHNIC BACKGROUND?: MOTHER - BLACK, AMERICAN INDIAN. - FATHER - WHITE (WELSH)

DO YOU HAVE A BOYFRIEND OR GIRLFRIEND? HOW LONG HAVE YOU TWO BEEN TOGETHER? WHERE DO YOU SEE THE RELATIONSHIP GOING? WHAT DRIVES YOU CRAZY ABOUT THE OTHER PERSON? WHAT'S THE BEST THING ABOUT THE OTHER PERSON? I HAVE JUST BROKEN UP (3 WEEKS AGO) WITH MY BOYFRIEND PAUL OF 3½ YEARS. WE ULTIMATELY FOUND IT TOO DIFFICULT TO DATE FROM 7,000 MILES. HE LEFT YESTERDAY AFTER A WEEKS' VISIT AND DROVE ME INSANE BECAUSE OF HIS COMPLETE LACK OF SPONTANEITY AND INITIATIVE. ONE MORE GORMLESS LOOK AND I WAS READY TO MAKE HIM SLEEP IN THE CAR. HE IS OBSESSED WITH MONEY AND BUDGETING AND ALTHOUGH HE HAS A GOOD JOB AND LOADED PARENTS, TO THE POINT OF COMPLETELY SACRIFICING HIS SOCIAL LIFE. THIS WAS ONE OF THE REASONS I LEFT ENGLAND. HE IS, HOWEVER, NOT A BAD PERSON - HE IS THE BEST BOYFRIEND I EVER HAD: VERY KIND, ATTENTIVE, LOVING, BRIGHT, EDUCATED, TACTILE (THOUGH RARELY IN PUBLIC), UNDERSTANDING. THESE THINGS I MISS.

DO YOU PLAY ANY SPORTS? I WAS A TRACK ATHLETE FOR A NUMBER OF YEARS BUT NEW LOCATIONS ETC HAVE MADE THIS DIFFICULT. I ALWAYS DABBLE IN GYM WORK (FREE WEIGHTS ETC), BUT HAVE JUST PURCHASED A NEW PAIR OF SPIKES AND FOUND A TRACK, SO I'M FEELING POSITIVE. I ALSO ENJOY BADMINTON, CYCLING, VOLLEYBALL, HOCKEY, HIGH-BOARD DIVING. I HAVE NEVER BEEN ABLE TO PLAY TENNIS.

WHAT ARE YOUR FAVORITE MUSICAL GROUPS / ARTISTS? I LIKE TO THINK MY TASTES ARE V. VARIED, BUT I AM AN 80's GIRL AT HEART. I ADORE GEORGE MICHAEL, LOVE SOUL, MOTOWN, ARETHA, THE VERVE, THE POLICE, MADONNA ETC. PROBABLY EASIEST TO SAY I CAN'T STAND COUNTRY OR HEAVY METAL.

OTHER SEXUAL ORIENTATIONS? THE MORE THE MERRIER

IF YOU COULD CHANGE ANY ONE THING ABOUT THE WAY YOU LOOK, WHAT WOULD THAT BE? MY CHIN - I THINK IT'S GOING TO DOUBLE LATER IN LIFE.

DO YOU: SMOKE CIGARETTES? DRINK ALCOHOL? HOW OLD WERE YOU WHEN YOU HAD YOUR FIRST DRINK? HOW MUCH DO YOU DRINK NOW? HOW OFTEN? SOCIALLY, BUT INCREASINGLY LESS WITH MEALS AS A FAMILY FROM AGE 13. DRINK WITH FRIENDS: 16, FIRST FULL SESSION: 17. NOW I DRINK SOCIALLY AT WEEKENDS, BUT MODERATELY. FIRST FULL BLOWN DRINK - TIL-I-PUKE AS HANGOVERS FAR TOO PAINFUL. FIRST REAL (DILUTED). WE DRANK WINE

IF YOU HAD ALADDIN'S LAMP AND THREE WISHES, WHAT WOULD THEY BE? 1. To live a long, painful, fulfilling and useful life. 2. TO SEE GEORGE MICHAEL IN CONCERT, FRONT ROW, MEET HIM, HAVE DINNER. HE'D FEBOWLED OVER BY LOOKS & WIT, AND WE'D HAVE A WILD NIGHT OF SEX (HE ALSO WOULDN'T BE GAY THIS PARTICULAR EVENING). 3. NO MORE NASTY AIDS.

Casting PIGGY

PIGGY: I live in Marin County, where there aren't a lot of young people. I guess that might be one reason that the show was appealing to me—that I might actually hang around people my age. Not to mention the fact that everything in my life was going downhill: I had my little sister living with me, which made me feel totally overwhelmed; I had a relationship I wasn't too thrilled with; and I was at a job that wasn't entirely fulfilling.

I waited until the very last second to send off my video. I never thought they'd ever call me. When they did, to

say I was shocked, well, that would be a complete understatement. The interview process was a total mind f**k. Telling all of this intimate information to people you don't know is very confusing. I'm very wary of people who pretend they like you when they don't know you, and I guess you could say that's what the whole casting process is about.

When I found out I had made it, I went mad. I was at work, and I just crouched under my desk, laughing and screaming and crying. I tried to look composed, but really I was shaking all over. It was quite a sight, and I'm not sure my office mates knew quite what to do with me.

IF YOU COULD ONLY PACK ONE BACKPACK FOR THE TRIP, WHAT WOULD BE IN IT?

#1 Toothbrush #2 Socks/Underwear #3 Couple good books
#4 good cigar #5 pants/shorts #6 few shirts
#7 cards #8 Jacket #9 Cap #10 X-tra shoes #11 first-aid

DESCRIBE YOUR MOST EMBARRASSING MOMENT.

Picture this. 8th grade young, popular, captain of soccer team, honor roll, and I'm running for class president. I was at the podium and as I started my speech, I started puberty. My voice could not stop cracking — not one sentence! ↑↓↑↓ it sounded as if I were testing the sound system. Suffice to say, every one was laughing, and I turned a nice shade of rouge.

HOW IMPORTANT IS SEX TO YOU? DO YOU HAVE IT ONLY WHEN YOU'RE IN A RELATIONSHIP OR DO YOU SEEK IT OUT AT OTHER TIMES? WHAT'S THE MOST EXCITING/INTERESTING PLACE YOU'VE EVER HAD SEX?

I love sex, I would like sex all the time — however it's not like that always in a relationship. The most interesting place was when I became a member of the "Mile-High club." The most exciting was more the anticipation than the place — But I was in my car.

OTHER SEXUAL ORIENTATIONS?

I don't like the idea of homosexuality, but when it comes down to it, Human kindness comes 1st. People shouldn't judge, period.

DO YOU HAVE A BOYFRIEND OR GIRLFRIEND? (circle one) HOW DID YOU MEET? HOW LONG HAVE YOU BEEN TOGETHER? WHAT DRIVES YOU CRAZY ABOUT THE OTHER PERSON? WHAT IS THE BEST THING ABOUT THE OTHER PERSON?

I met her through a former roommate of mine. He was a waiter, and she was a waitress. The second he saw her, he knew she was "Chadwick" type. He arranged it all; we met at a local bowling joint, the rest is history." We've been together for 2 years in January '98. Her name is Sky, and I love her, but she neglects her work-outs, she likes to be right all the time, she's pushing marriage (MAIS NON!) and she wants my kids in Hebrew school (z) But you know what? Her heart beat puts me to sleep atnight, she feeds me, she loves me, she respects me — and she doesn't get angry if I make comment about other women!

CHADWICK TALKS BACK

CHADWICK: In the casting special, they show me saying that I have libido coming out of my ears. Yes, that's true. And, yes, I said that. And I also said stuff about Sky's lack of sex drive. But come on! I spent hours and hours of time telling them how much I loved Sky, too, and that's what they showed? I called Sky after it aired, and she was really upset. I tried to explain. I knew that it hurt her. And, therefore, it hurt me.

WHAT IS THE MOST IMPORTANT ISSUE OR PROBLEM FACING YOU TODAY?

Career probably... You know (SCHOOL, MAKE $) ← → (HAVE FUN, LIVE LIFE TO THE FULLEST) I don't look at it as a problem but a tough decision. I want to be a great support for my family.

Casting CHADWICK

CHADWICK: I was watching the <u>Road Rules</u> Islands show, and I thought, "That's it. I want to do this. I love a good adventure."

I didn't even apply. I just randomly called the Bunim-Murray offices and asked for the casting department. They told me to make a video. Well, I didn't want to make a video; it just wouldn't represent me. So I knew what I had to do. I had to go there and show myself. The woman from the casting department thought it was pretty audacious, my showing up there out of the blue. She told me to fill out a casting application and send it back. I filled it out, but I just brought it back in person the next day. Pretty bold. I don't think they could believe it. I had to plead with them: "Come on, I did the application. Why don't you just shoot an interview with me now?"

All my interviews were about Sky, my girlfriend. It was like that was all anybody cared about. It got frustrating to me—all these hours and hours talking about Sky. Finally, I just confronted them. "You know what? Sky's not going on the trip. I am. If you have any questions for me and about me, I'd be happy to answer them."

I always wanted to do <u>Road Rules</u>. I never wanted to do <u>The Real World</u>. But Mary-Ellis, one of the executive producers, wanted me for <u>The Real World</u>. She kept trying to sell me on Seattle. She called me at work, and we talked for forty minutes. "I don't want to put my life on hold for six months," I told her. "My heart's set on going on the road."

So <u>Road Rules</u> it was. I heard later that the <u>Real World</u> house in Seattle had an indoor gym and a rock wall. I had to wonder if I'd made the right choice.

Casting KEFLA

KEFLA: It was crazy from the start. My roommate at Alabama State University was working in the student-activities department, and he told me that MTV was coming to town. He was actually taking some MTV folk out to dinner and invited me to come. I kept them laughing the whole time. I told them about how I used to be the school mascot, Horny the Hornet; how I used to battle with the Arkansas Pine Bluff; about my family—all kinds of stuff. At the end of the meal, they were like, "Would you ever consider doing our show <u>Road Rules</u>?"

I filled out an application and did an interview with them. A few days later, I got a call. "You made it to the finals!" What? Then they asked me: "So, how does it feel to have skipped the process?"

I was like, "What??? What do you mean 'the process'? What is the process?" I had no idea I'd had it so easy.

There wasn't much time between finals and going on the road, and I used it to brush up on my <u>Road Rules</u> and <u>Real World</u>. I watched a few marathons. I dug Kameelah from <u>The Real World-Boston</u>. And I really got into Roni from <u>Road Rules-Northern Trail</u>. But I got to see only a couple of shows before it was time to go.

EXCERPTS FROM KEFLA'S CASTING APPLICATION.

WHAT DO YOU DO FOR FUN?
For fun, I like to hang-out with my fellow cheerleaders (I'm the school Mascot) and go to the mall. I also go to the Bowling Alley with my FRAT Brothers.

WHAT ARE YOUR FAVORITE MUSICAL GROUPS/ARTISTS?
A Tribe Called Quest / Prince / New Edition / Eryka Badu / Busta Rhymes / Fugee / Buju Banton / Bob Marley

WHERE DO YOU WORK? DESCRIBE YOUR JOB HISTORY:
American Eagle Outfitters - Montgomery Mall   Held Seasonal Jobs
@ Reebok, Guess, Starter, and Tommy Hilfiger outlet Stores in Foley Alabama

DESCRIBE HOW CONFLICTS WERE HANDLED AT HOME AS YOU WERE GROWING UP (WHO WOULD WIN AND WHO WOULD LOSE, WHETHER THERE WAS YELLING OR HITTING, ETC.)?
Whenever there was a conflict between my brothers and I my parents would step in and give us a "whipping" for fighting. We were never abused, just your "good 'ole' fashion" "ass whooping".

IF YOU HAVE ANY BROTHERS OR SISTERS, ARE YOU CLOSE? HOW WOULD YOU DESCRIBE YOUR RELATIONSHIP WITH THEM?
My relationship with my Brothers is very close. I would go to hell and Back for my Brothers and I'm sure they would do the same for me.

WHAT ARE YOUR PERSONAL (NOT CAREER) GOALS IN LIFE?
1) Live my life to the fullest with out any regrets. 2) Get a closer relationship with God, Family and Friends. 3) Save enough money and assets so that once I'm dead those that I've left behind will be well taken care of

HOW WOULD SOMEONE WHO REALLY KNOWS YOU DESCRIBE YOUR WORST TRAITS? They would say "Sometimes he can be overly excited, too playful, and too trustworthy. He also procrastinates at times"

DESCRIBE YOUR FANTASY DATE Arriving at my dates house with 6 Roses in my hand. One for each hour that we spend together. Every hour on the hour I'll give her a rose and explain to her how beautiful she is. Will go out to eat and later come back to my house where I'll ask her to help me fold my clothes.

HOW DID YOUR PARENTS TREAT EACH OTHER? (DID YOUR PARENTS HAVE A GOOD MARRIAGE? WHAT WAS IT LIKE?)
My parents marriage was a perfect marriage. There was so much love around that it carried over to the children. My brothers and I are so caring and loving, and we owe it all to the way our parents were / are in their marriage.

DO YOU HAVE ANY HABITS WE SHOULD KNOW ABOUT?
I like to watch T.V., Surf the Net, and exercise.

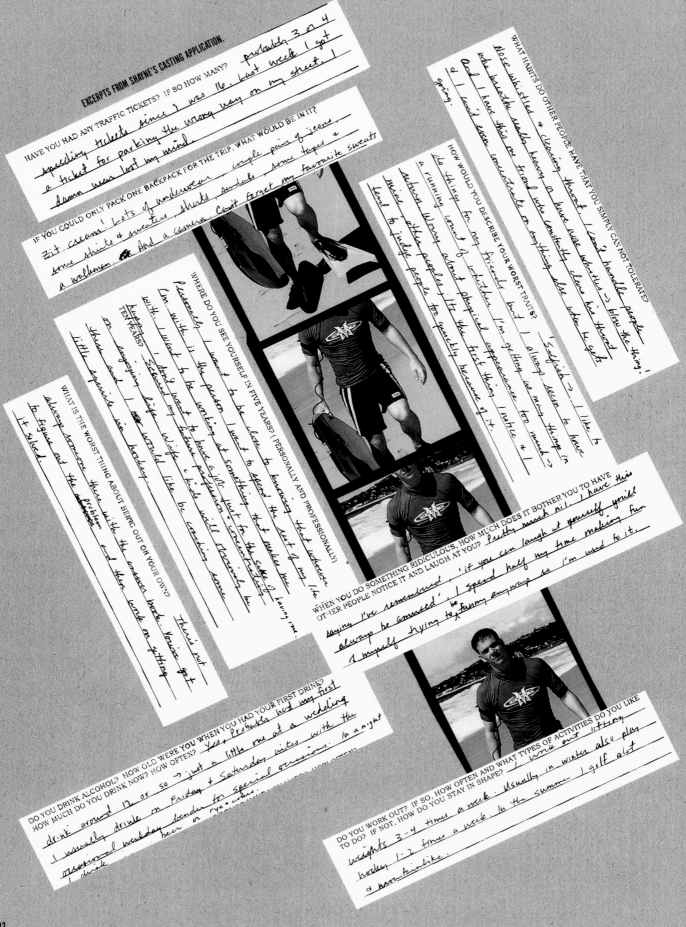

HAVE YOU HAD ANY TRAFFIC TICKETS? IF SO HOW MANY? probably 3 or 4 speeding tickets since I was 16. Last week I got a ticket for parking the wrong way on my street. I damn near lost my mind.

IF YOU COULD ONLY PACK ONE BACKPACK FOR THE TRIP, WHAT WOULD BE IN IT? Lots of underwear, couple pair of jeans, zit cream! some shirts & sweaters, sandals, some tapes & a walkman and a camera. Can't forget my favorite sweats.

WHAT HABITS DO OTHER PEOPLE HAVE THAT YOU SIMPLY CAN NOT TOLERATE? Nose whistles & chewing. I have this one friend who constantly clears his throat & I have this one friend who breathes really heavy & another who breath whistles → blows the thing! and I can't even concentrate on anything else when he gets going.

HOW WOULD YOU DESCRIBE YOUR WORST TRAITS? "Selfish" → I like to do things for my friends but I'm getting at most things in return → I always seem to hear myself. A running worry about whether it's the first thing I notice & I tend to judge people too quickly because of it. Whether other peoples life the physical experience is when I think about physical experience.

WHERE DO YOU SEE YOURSELF IN FIVE YEARS? (PERSONALLY AND PROFESSIONALLY) Personally, I want to be close to knowing that whatever I'm with is the person I want to spend the rest of my life with. I want to have a girlfriend & concentrate on keeping it. I don't want to have a high profession that makes me scared my future wife & kids will eventually be on everything like crazy. Professionally be keeping on in hockey.

WHEN YOU DO SOMETHING RIDICULOUS, HOW MUCH DOES IT BOTHER YOU TO HAVE OTHER PEOPLE NOTICE IT AND LAUGH AT YOU? Pretty much nil. I have this saying I've remembered, "if you can laugh at yourself, you'll always be amused". I spend half my time making fun of myself trying to be funny anyways so I'm used to it.

WHAT IS THE WORST THING ABOUT BEING OUT ON YOUR OWN? always seems there is some problem and then work on getting to figure out the next one and then work on getting it solved. There's not. You've got

DO YOU DRINK ALCOHOL? HOW OLD WERE YOU WHEN YOU HAD YOUR FIRST DRINK? HOW MUCH DO YOU DRINK NOW? HOW OFTEN? Yes, Probably had my first drink around 12 or so → just a little one at a wedding. I usually drink on Friday & Saturday nites with the occasional weekday bender for special occasions. In a night I drink beer or rye-cokes.

DO YOU WORK OUT? IF SO, HOW OFTEN AND WHAT TYPES OF ACTIVITIES DO YOU LIKE TO DO? IF NOT, HOW DO YOU STAY IN SHAPE? I work out lifting weights 3-4 times a week. Usually in winter also play hockey 1-2 times a week. In the summer I golf alot & mountainbike.

Casting SHAYNE

SHAYNE: How does a Canadian get on Road Rules?

Well, I was down in Memphis, visiting some friends of mine. We were watching some episodes of this MTV show where kids run around Europe competing in activities, and I was like, "What is this? This is awesome!" My friends thought I'd be great for it and told me I should apply. Of course, they didn't tell me that it was more of a soap opera than a sports–and–adventure competition. Really, that's what I thought it was going to be.

So when I got back home, I borrowed a camera from a friend, went down to the basement, and made a video. I tried to do some fun stuff. I did some weight–lifter poses and a couple of dance steps. I'm not your average white guy. I've got rhythm. I've got the moves.

But, despite my moves, about a week after I turned in the tape, I got a P.F.O. letter. That's short for "Please F**k Off." They said they weren't casting at the moment, but they'd get back to me when they were. I figured that was a total lie and that I'd never hear from them again.

Well, wasn't I surprised when four months later I got a call saying I'd made it to semifinals? I really had no idea what the casting people wanted when they interviewed me. I don't have any sob stories. I guess what they liked about me was that I'm a little green. There aren't many black people in my town; I know only one homosexual. I'm in squaresville here. Basically, I'm a meatball. But I'm an open–minded meatball.

DESCRIBE YOUR MOST EMBARRASSING MOMENT.

Last year when I was living in Oxford, the dorm caught on fire. The whole building was evacuated - except me. I was naked in the shower. The Fire Brigade wouldn't allow me access to my room and so I stood outside in winter, in a towel and cow slippers, in front of the neighborhood. It was funny, but as I laughed on the outside, I was ready to cry on the inside.

WHERE DO YOU SEE YOURSELF IN FIVE YEARS? WHAT IS YOUR CAREER GOAL?

Teaching Philosophy at the Sorbonne, in Paris. I want to be one of the few women to go down in Philosophy history. Or be a rockstar.

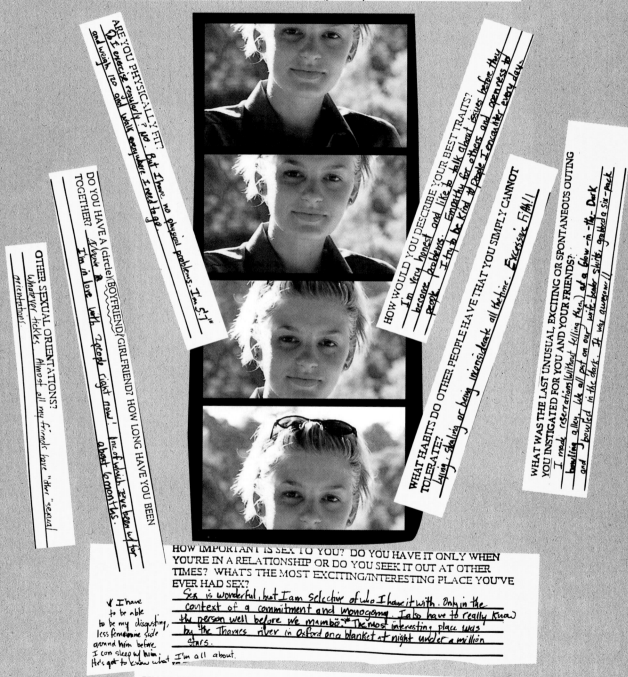

ARE YOU PHYSICALLY FIT? Do I exercise regularly? No. But I have no physical problems. I'm 5'7" and weigh 120 and I walk everywhere I need to go.

DO YOU HAVE A (circle) BOYFRIEND/GIRLFRIEND? HOW LONG HAVE YOU BEEN TOGETHER? I have a boyfriend. I'm in love with 2 people right now. One of which I've been w/ for about 6 months.

OTHER SEXUAL ORIENTATIONS? Whatever tickles. Almost all my friends have "other" sexual orientations.

HOW WOULD YOU DESCRIBE YOUR BEST TRAITS? I'm very honest and like to talk about issues before they become problems. Empathy for others and openness to people. I try to be kind to people I encounter every day.

WHAT HABITS DO OTHER PEOPLE HAVE THAT YOU SIMPLY CANNOT TOLERATE? Lying, stealing or being inconsiderate all the time. Excessive E-mail.

WHAT WAS THE LAST UNUSUAL, EXCITING OR SPONTANEOUS OUTING YOU INSTIGATED FOR YOU AND YOUR FRIENDS? I made reservations (without telling them) at a blow-in-the-Dark bowling alley. We all got on our white-body shirts, grabbed a six-pack and bowled in the dark. It was awesome!!

HOW IMPORTANT IS SEX TO YOU? DO YOU HAVE IT ONLY WHEN YOU'RE IN A RELATIONSHIP OR DO YOU SEEK IT OUT AT OTHER TIMES? WHAT'S THE MOST EXCITING/INTERESTING PLACE YOU'VE EVER HAD SEX?

Sex is wonderful, but I am selective of who I have it with. Only in the context of a commitment and monogamy. I also have to really know the person well before we mambo* The most interesting place was by the Thames river in Oxford on a blanket at night under a million stars.

*I have to be able to be my disgusting, less feminine side around him before I can sleep w/ him. He's got to know what I'm all about.

TELL US ABOUT SOME PLACES IN THE UNITED STATES YOU HAVE ALWAYS WISHED YOU COULD VISIT AND WHY?

I've always wanted to live in New York. Since I was 7 years old, New York has been my dream. I'm also curious about the mid-west, and the South. Particularly Tennessee and Louisiana, b/c I have friends from there.

Casting CHRISTINA

CHRISTINA: They had a casting call for <u>The Real World</u> right in my school cafeteria. It was the biggest group of geeks I'd ever seen. They were all sucking up to the casting directors. It was pathetic. "Pick me! Pick me!"

I just started talking to one of the women from casting. I was being a bitch, but I guess she liked me, because she gave me an application, interviewed me, and asked me to come back.

I was much more inclined toward <u>The Real World</u> than <u>Road Rules</u>. I didn't want to do <u>Road Rules</u>. It seemed kind

of like a surrealistic game show to me. Sort of sadistic too. I just don't see the fun in being tortured. I'm not athletic at all. I would much rather sit in a house for six months.

The casting interviews really threw me. They're tedious. You get asked all sorts of questions. "What do you have for breakfast? When did you have your first sexual thought?" It's grueling.

When I found out I got <u>Road Rules</u> and not <u>The Real World</u>, well, it was kind of a disappointment. But at least I knew I was headed for a challenge.

Casting SUSIE

DESCRIBE A TYPICAL FRIDAY OR SATURDAY NIGHT *WORK - WORK - WORK. ALL MY FRIENDS WENT AWAY TO COLLEGE & I'M STUCK HERE AT COMMUNITY COLLEGE SO I WORK*

HOW OLD WERE YOU WHEN YOU HAD YOUR FIRST DRINK? HOW MUCH DO YOU DRINK NOW? HOW OFTEN? *I'VE NEVER HAD ALCOHOL.*

OTHER SEXUAL ORIENTATIONS? *I DON'T AGREE WITH HOMOSEXUALITY, BUT NOBODY DESERVES TO BE TREATED BADLY BECAUSE OF IT. I GUESS IT'S A "LOVE THE SINNER; HATE THE SIN" TYPE PHILOSOPHY.*

WHAT DO YOU DO FOR FUN? *ANYTHING THAT IS NOT SELF DESTRUCTIVE.*

DO YOU HAVE ANY HABITS WE SHOULD KNOW ABOUT? *I SING CONSTANTLY...24-7... I CAN'T STOP MYSELF. I LOVE MUSIC. I HAVE A LIONEL RICHIE SONG STUCK IN MY HEAD TODAY - ITS PAINFUL.*

SUSIE: I went from being an obsessive Road Rules fan to actually getting on the show. Amazing. It was like I cracked the system. I turned 18 and was like, "It's time." So I borrowed my sister's camera, made a tape, and sent it in. Three days later, they called me. Who knew it would be that easy?

I flirted my way through the semifinals interview. About ten minutes into it, I interrupted the interviewer. "Is that your natural eye color?" I asked him. There was a girl who was also interviewing me, but I kept ignoring her. Finally, she was like, "Hello, I'm here too." What can I say? I'm a flirt.

WHERE DO YOU WORK? DESCRIBE YOUR JOB HISTORY: BLOCKBUSTER MUSIC, NIGHTS + WEEKENDS + I HOSTESS AT CHILE'S RESTAURANT WEEKDAYS. I'VE BEEN WORKING SINCE I WAS 13. I WORKED AT A FRUIT + VEGETABLE MARKET FOR 4 YEARS + GOT THE PRESENT JOBS RECENTLY. I DESPISE LAZY PEOPLE FOR THIS VERY REASON.

IN YOUR OPINION, WHAT ARE THE GREATEST PROBLEMS AND CHALLENGES FACING KIDS WHO ARE GROWING UP TODAY? THE BIGGEST PROBLEM IN MY OPINION IS NOT DRUGS, OR PEER PRESSURE, IT'S ATTITUDE. LIFE IS 90% HOW WE REACT TO THINGS + ONLY 10% WHAT HAPPENS TO US. TEENS NEED A NEW PERSPECTIVE + ATTITUDE BEFORE WE CAN MAKE ANY POSITIVE CHANGES. IGNORANCE IS ANOTHER BIG ONE - MYSELF INCLUDED.

DESCRIBE YOUR FANTASY DATE BEING WITH SOMEONE WHO THOUGHT EVERYTHING I DID WAS MAGICAL HELLO, SLEEPLESS IN SEATTLE, ALERT!?!

1-10-98
  GOD IS SO GOOD. AS I PUSHED THE "PLAY" BUTTON ON MY ANSWERING MACHINE THAT FATEFUL OCTOBER DAY LITTLE DID I KNOW WHAT WOULD SOON FILL MY EARS. THE VOICE ON THE TAPE SAID IT WAS REBO FROM "REAL WORLD" CASTING. HOW COULD THIS BE?!? BUT IT WAS, AND THUS BEGAN THE JOURNEY OF A LIFETIME. I HAVE NO IDEA WHAT GOD HAS IN STORE FOR ME, BUT HE WILL DO GREAT THINGS. I HAVE NO CONTROL OVER THE PATH ON WHICH HE LEADS ME, BUT HE KNOWS WHAT IS BEST IN MY LIFE AND THE LIVES WHICH I WILL COME IN CONTACT WITH. I WANT TO SPREAD THE LIGHT OF JESUS

SUSIE'S DAIRY

HOW IMPORTANT IS SEX TO YOU? DO YOU HAVE IT ONLY WHEN YOU'RE IN A RELATIONSHIP OR DO YOU SEEK IT OUT AT OTHER TIMES? HOW DID IT COME ABOUT ON THE LAST OCCASION? I'VE NEVER HAD SEX. IT'S NOT A BIG ISSUE - I DON'T GO SCREAMIN' IT ON ROOFTOPS. BUT I MADE A CONSCIOUS DECISION TO WAIT TILL MARRIAGE. IT'S A BIG CONFLICT OF INTERESTS THOUGH, BECAUSE OF MY LOVE FOR MEN. MY MORAL STANDARDS DO PREVAIL IN THE END. IT WOULD BE HARDER TO ABSTAIN IF I WAS IN LOVE BUT I'VE NEVER HAD THAT EMOTIONAL BOND W/ SOMEONE.

IS THERE ANY ISSUE, POLITICAL OR SOCIAL, THAT YOU'RE PASSIONATE ABOUT? HAVE YOU DONE ANYTHING ABOUT IT? MY BIGGEST POLITICAL ISSUE IS THE PRO-LIFE MOVEMENT. I RESPECT ALL VIEWS, BUT I'M PRO-LIFE. I'VE GONE TO MARCHES & RALLIES. NOTHING EXTREME OR VIOLENT, THAT'S UNECESSARY. I WANT TO MEET PEOPLE W/ OTHER VIEWS THAT'S ANOTHER REASON I WANT TO BE ON THE REAL WORLD.

DO YOU EVER PLAN TO HAVE CHILDREN OF YOUR OWN? IF SO, WHEN AND HOW MANY? HECK NO!!! MY MOM BABYSITS IN OUR HOME + I'VE SEEN THE GOOD, THE BAD, + THE UGLY. THEY'RE NOTHIN' BUT TROUBLE.

Road Rules VI

CHADWICK

CHRISTINA

SUSIE ### KEFLA ### PIGGY ### SHAYNE

With Special Appearances by
DAN and TARA from NORTHERN TRAIL
GEOFF, the AUSSIE DRIVING INSTRUCTOR
CHRISTIAN and TIMMY from Season Two
The cast of THE REAL WORLD-SEATTLE:
LINDSAY, JANET, DAVID,

STEPHEN, REBECCA, and NATHAN
THE CROC CATCHERS
A BRIGADE of FIRE FIGHTERS,
The REPORTERS at the WEEKLY WORLD NEWS
SOME FOXY LIFEGUARDS, and...

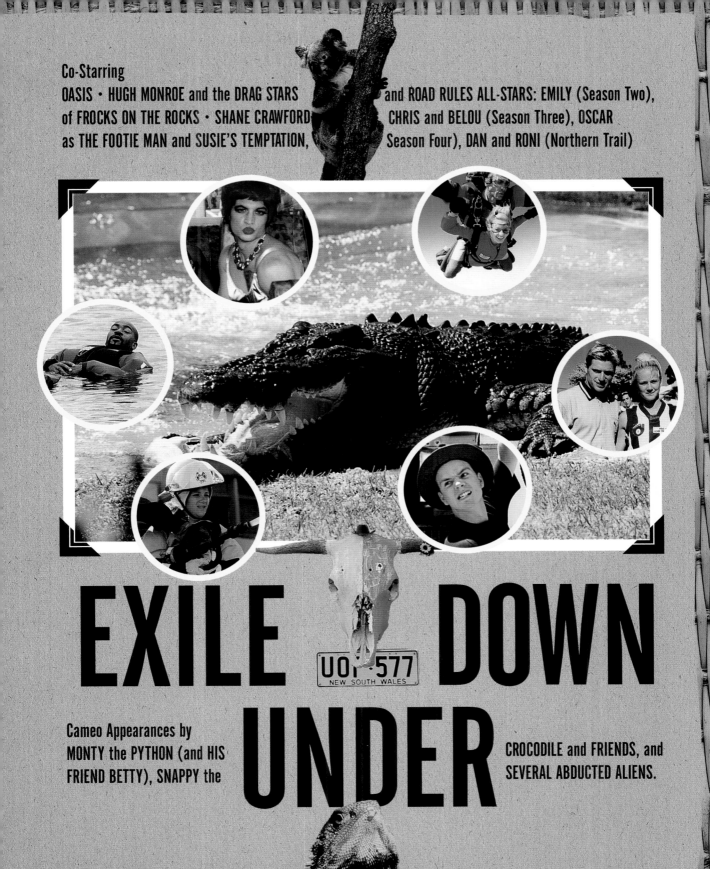

Co-Starring

OASIS • HUGH MONROE and the DRAG STARS of FROCKS ON THE ROCKS • SHANE CRAWFORD as THE FOOTIE MAN and SUSIE'S TEMPTATION, and ROAD RULES ALL-STARS: EMILY (Season Two), CHRIS and BELOU (Season Three), OSCAR (Season Four), DAN and RONI (Northern Trail)

EXILE DOWN UNDER

UO1·577
NEW SOUTH WALES

Cameo Appearances by
MONTY the PYTHON (and HIS FRIEND BETTY), SNAPPY the CROCODILE and FRIENDS, and SEVERAL ABDUCTED ALIENS.

FIRST IMPRESSIONS

MISSION

Aloha, Road Rules VI cast! Dive right into the adventure of your lives!

SHAYNE'S DIARY

The ride to Waimea Beach was about an hour, and I've never been so excited in my life. I am so curious as to who the rest of the cast is, what they're doing, what they look like. On the ride, the driver went back and forth on the same stretch for a while, and it was right at the famous North Shore. I thought we were surfing for sure. Then they told me to lie down in the back seat, and about two minutes later the car stopped and we were there. I got out and got my back pack on, spotted Susie and headed over. I was so nervous. Two months of preparation and I couldn't believe I was finally doing it. I was smitten right off the bat with Susie, but also a little apprehensive. She started babbling, and I had sensory overload just trying to figure out what was going on. Piggy was next, and I'm thinking, She's gonna be fun. Anytime British people start talking, I usually laugh especially when they swear and talk trash. Kefla walks up, and I had expected a black cast member, but for some reason I just thought we'd have this dreadlocked guy, so I'm thrown for a loop. By the time Christina walked up, my mind was racing a hundred miles a minute. Chadwick appears, and he seems really "together" to me, except I can't figure out why he's wearing jeans.

SUSIE: My first impressions of everybody

SHAYNE is a babelicious Canadian. **PIGGY** is an over-the-top, witty little thing. **KEFLA** is a cool, calm, collected, mellow kind of fellow. **CHADWICK'S** a leader who's confident and self-assured. And **CHRISTINA'S** a mad-at-the-world alternative punk who's not going to like me.

LOVE ON THE ROCKS

KEFLA: I was hoping they were going to hook me up with a person of color. When I got to the bridge, I realized that wasn't going to happen. I was not going to be connecting with anyone in a boy-girl kinda way.

CHADWICK: When I got to the bridge, I was like "Oh." Susie is the furthest thing from my type. She's not stupid; she's just young. At first I thought Christina was cute. All of the girls are fine. None of them have bad bodies. But from the start I knew it'd be like hanging out with sisters. It was so funny. That first day, Susie was lounging around for the cameras in these Sports Illustrated-style poses. I'll bet there will be tons of people who'll say she's gorgeous, but once you live with someone like that, you stop seeing it.

THE RETURN OF DAN AND TARA

TARA: Dan and I had fun in Hawaii. Of course, it probably would have been more fun if we'd still been going out, but what can you do? We stayed in the same room and slept in the same bed—just for old time's sake. But we didn't do anything. We were both like, "Dang! We didn't get any!"

DAN: I have to admit, I was jealous of the new Road Rules cast. Their trip was just starting, and mine was already over.

BATHING BEAUTIES

CHRISTINA: Straight off the bat, Piggy and I developed a massive insecurity about Susie's cuteness. And it didn't make things better that on the first day of the trip we had to be in our bathing suits. It was traumatic to be on a cliff in a bikini with cameras glaring at you. Everyone was checking one another out. And Susie's just blonde, with long legs and a great body. She said she did ab roller for months before the show. And Piggy said she spent months with a trainer before coming on the show. I'm completely out of shape.

PIGGY: That was a nasty thing for them to do, putting us in bathing suits on the first day. I admit, I'd been training pretty hard. But thank God I did: I was the biggest girl there. On that first day, we had to walk up the cliff, asses everywhere. By the way, we were given those bikinis. That Christina and I picked the same one was a total coincidence.

WHAT KEFLA PACKED

KEFLA: I packed a few special things for this trip. I brought a book called Acts of Faith. I read a different act every day just to keep me motivated. I also packed my clipper to keep myself shaved and to keep my hair fresh. I got my hair tonic, my little scalp cleanser, my scalp moisturizer and replenisher, so after I shave, my head won't be dry. I like to keep that nice little Isaac Hayes look, I guess you could say.

SHAYNE: Here's a random thought from day one: I was the token skinny guy. I worked out regularly before the show, but when I took off my shirt, I discovered I was easily the smallest guy. A brutal realization, and we were only a half hour into the show!

CHRISTINA TALKS BACK

CHRISTINA: I feel like I need to defend the way I was on the first day, which was really quiet. But I was taken aback. Everyone was so buddy-buddy so quickly. They were just acting like best friends. I know they thought I had an attitude, and it's probably going to look like that on the show. I was quiet because it seemed so phony to me. I didn't know what to do.

GOING DOWN

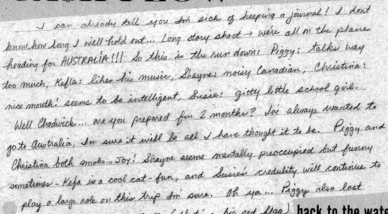

THE LOST EPISODE OF ROAD RULES VI

PIGGY'S CA$H FLOW

FROM CHADWICK'S DIARY

I can already tell you I'm sick of keeping a journal! I don't know how long I will hold out... Long story short → we're all on the plane heading for AUSTRALIA!!! So this is the run down: Piggy: talks way too much, Kefa: likes his music, Shayne: noisy Canadian, Christina: nice mouth, seems to be intelligent, Susie: giddy little school girl. Well Chadwick... are you prepared for 2 months? I've always wanted to go to Australia, I'm sure it will be all I have thought it to be. Piggy and Christina both smoke... JOY! Shayne seems mentally preoccupied but funny sometimes - Kefa is a cool cat - fun, and Susie's credulity will continue to play a large role on this trip I'm sure. Oh ya ... Piggy also lost her money already... + 300⁰⁰ (that's a big red flag)

PIGGY: Perhaps they've spared me by not actually showing this on television, but on the first day of our trip, I lost $300. Yes, $300. After our first mission, we each got envelopes of money. Well, we stuffed them in the bag, went off to the beach, did our search for buried treasure, got ready to go out for a meal, because we were absolutely starving. So we're about to get into the van to go to the restaurant, and I go to check my money, and what do you know, I appeared to have lost it. I think the confusion resulted from when we were at the falls, I said to Shayne, "Do you have the money?" He said, "Yes." Well, he meant the extra $300 we'd won for doing the 45-footer. I don't know why I presumed he had my personal cash, but it wasn't on the beach when I looked for it, so it just made sense to me.

Thank God, we made a mad dash back to the waterfalls, and Art was there with my money. What a relief.

Then it happened again. We were getting off the plane in Australia. We were all feeling a little dozy, a little dopey from the flight. We were standing in baggage claim, and we decided to exchange $50 so we could travel to the youth hostel. I checked my bags, and my money was gone. I didn't know what to do. I was completely embarrassed and feeling like a complete flake. I was just sick to my stomach. We were standing around searching for ages, and then we realized that I'd mistakenly put my money in Christina's bag. She took it out and put it in her back pocket. So I didn't have to carry anything.

Obviously, I'm really bad with money. It's not that I'm a big-spending girl, it's just that it disappears.

SHAYNE: I can't for the life of me understand why Piggy thought I would take her money right off the bat and just hold on to it. It pissed me off.

KEFLA: Dang! We couldn't go a day without this girl losing her money. I was like, "Look, someone needs to hold this girl's money." "Cut it," I said. "Don't let her have her own money until she's ready to buy something!"

WHAT PIGGY WOULD GO ON TO LOSE:
Her passport
Her hair-care products
Her bathing suit
Her towel
Her sunglasses
Susie's sunglasses
Her patience on the road
Her bet with Chadwick that she couldn't stop cursing
Numerous room keys

SUSIE

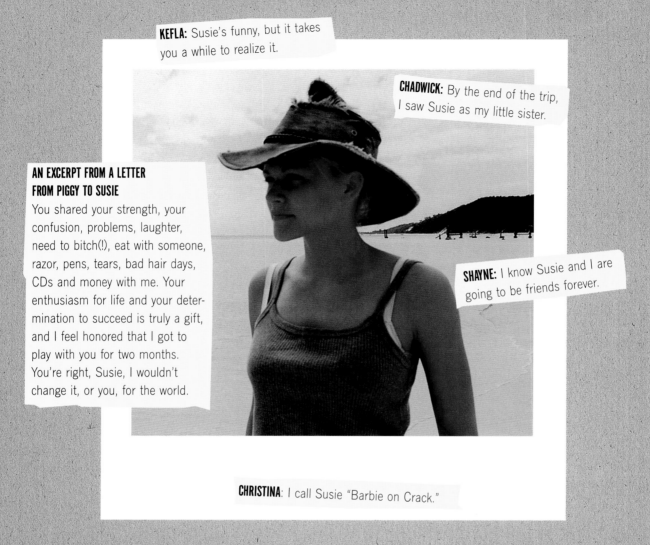

KEFLA: Susie's funny, but it takes you a while to realize it.

CHADWICK: By the end of the trip, I saw Susie as my little sister.

AN EXCERPT FROM A LETTER FROM PIGGY TO SUSIE

You shared your strength, your confusion, problems, laughter, need to bitch(!), eat with someone, razor, pens, tears, bad hair days, CDs and money with me. Your enthusiasm for life and your determination to succeed is truly a gift, and I feel honored that I got to play with you for two months. You're right, Susie, I wouldn't change it, or you, for the world.

SHAYNE: I know Susie and I are going to be friends forever.

CHRISTINA: I call Susie "Barbie on Crack."

SUSIE: In seventh grade, my best friend and I started relating everything in our lives to The Brady Bunch. The analogies are endless. My favorite Brady was Bobby. I'm not a Marcia fan. She was too obsessed with what people thought. But Bobby wasn't. You know the episode where Bobby was afraid of heights and then his parakeet flew out the window and he had to overcome his fears? Well, that's what going on Road Rules is like.

Road Rules breaks down every stereotype you have. I was the young one, the typical naive one. But I was forced to reevaluate my ideas, my religion, the way I act with guys. I changed so much, and honestly, I didn't expect to change at all.

You know, it's funny. Before you go on the road, the producers tell you it's going to be rough. But you don't believe them. It goes in one ear and out the other. But living so closely with other people—not to mention cameras—was just extraordinary.

SUSIE TELLS YOU HOW THE BRADY BUNCH CAST
IS LIKE THE ROAD RULES VI CAST

GREG: Played guitar in high school to impress girls
Went into medicine
Appeared on Hal Burton's TV Talent Review

CHADWICK: Played guitar in elevator to impress Piggy
Went into medicine (paramedic)
Appeared on Beverly Hills 90210

PETER: Offensive end on football team
Did a magic act for vaudeville show
Eats pork chops and applesauce

KEFLA: Mascot for football team
Did a drag-queen act for gay and lesbian Mardi Gras
Eats fried chicken and grits

BOBBY: Bitter about losing "Golden Scoop" ice cream eating contest
Gave Millicent "niceys" in backyard
Dumped water on Mike for Family Frolics act

SHAYNE: Bitter about losing fire-brigade fire-fighting contest
Gave Susie "niceys" in the back of the Winnie
Dumped water on Kefla for shrinkage in the shower

MARCIA: Had swollen nose after getting hit by a football
President of Davy Jones fan club
Did a song and dance with Carol for Family Frolics night

SUSIE: Had swollen ego after getting hit on by football player
President of Timmy from Road Rules II fan club
Did a song and dance with Piggy and Christina for money on the street

JAN: Wrecked bike in garage because she wouldn't wear her glasses
Sang lead vocals for The Silver Platters
Annoyed by overachieving elder sibling, Marcia

PIGGY: Wrecked Winnebago in gas station because she didn't pay attention
Sang lead vocals for Luscious Beaver
Annoyed by overachieving elder cast member, Chadwick

CINDY: Game-show contestant on Question the Kids. (lost)
Body double played by a midget
Awarded jacks for "Best Jacks Player at the Playground"

CHRISTINA: Game-show contestant on Dating Roulette (lost)
Mysterious phobia of midgets
Awarded shirt for "Best Lifesaver at Marcoola Beach"

Frocks on the Rocks

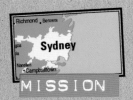

MISSION

Spice up your life as you swap genders and "Shoop Shoop" for millions.

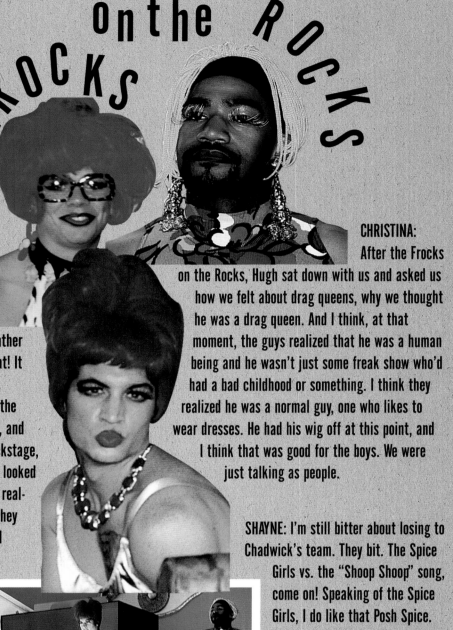

SUSIE: Frocks on the Rocks rocked my world. There was a theme song they kept playing: "Different is hard, different is lonely, different is trouble for you, only different is heartache. Different is pain, but I'd rather be different than be the same!" Love that! It became our favorite new song.

Here's something you didn't see on the show. We had just done our performance, and Kefla was still in his outfit. We were backstage, and this guy came up to him. He smiled, looked him up and down, then took a second to really survey the goods. "So it's true what they say about black men?" he said. I started laughing, but Kefla was so embarrassed.

PIGGY: The girls made up the boys. Susie did Chadwick's and Shayne's lips, and I have to say I was a little disappointed with Shayne's. I think, well, let's just say he didn't look too good. But, somehow, he made up for it. He really had the drag thing down as far as I'm concerned. Shayne is very in touch with his feminine side.

CHRISTINA: After the Frocks on the Rocks, Hugh sat down with us and asked us how we felt about drag queens, why we thought he was a drag queen. And I think, at that moment, the guys realized that he was a human being and he wasn't just some freak show who'd had a bad childhood or something. I think they realized he was a normal guy, one who likes to wear dresses. He had his wig off at this point, and I think that was good for the boys. We were just talking as people.

SHAYNE: I'm still bitter about losing to Chadwick's team. They bit. The Spice Girls vs. the "Shoop Shoop" song, come on! Speaking of the Spice Girls, I do like that Posh Spice.

You don't see this on the show, but we had an incredibly difficult time getting clothes together. Maybe it looks like it came easily to us, but, no, it did not. The guy who ran the store basically had to take us under his wing. I was very impressed when I realized everything drag queens go through. That's a lot of work.

PIGGY AND CHADWICK

PIGGY: It was around the time of Frocks on the Rocks that Chadwick started driving me mad. I guess it probably had something to do with the fact that I was so attracted to him at first. But I'm a bad judge of character. He just started to really annoy me. Chadwick thinks he's an old soul. As far as I'm concerned, the best thing you can know at 24 is that you've got a lot more to know. Well, Chadwick's 24, but he thinks he knows it all.

Those acrobatics that he did in the room? Here's why that started. Susie was going to do a handstand. She was preparing herself, looking really cute with her arms in the air. She was about to go over on her hands and knees, and Chadwick goes, "I'm learning backsprings." Why would he do that? To make her feel dumb, of course. And then he did some. Right there in the room. And he wonders why we call him Captain America?

CAPTAIN AMERICA

CHADWICK: I claim to not care what people say about me, but I never thought I'd feel so misperceived as I did on this trip. They called me Captain America. That really hurt. Captain America is a fictional character, and, hello, I'm a carbon-based life form. If I'm good at things, it doesn't make me a bad person. Leave me alone. It's just me.

CHADWICK TALKS BACK

CHADWICK: I knew they were going to make a big deal about me and Piggy and our supposed love-hate relationship. Looking back on that fight we had when I did the backflips, I realize I shouldn't have done them. I had nothing to prove to her.

OUR HOME DOWN UNDER

TRAFFIC SIGNS PORTION OF THE TE

1) This sign means –

A) Look out for kangaroos.
B) Kangaroos crossing ahead for 5 km.
C) Kangaroo lane. Kangaroos have right of way.

MISSION

Shift gears and change lanes! The Winnie is yours, but can you drive it? Time to get tested!

SHAYNE & SUSIE

Koalas, kangas, and snakes, oh my. Go wild, Road Rulers!

I'M THE ONLY ONE ON THE WHOLE TRIP WHO'S HOMESICK AND I FEEL LIKE AN IDIOT. EVERYONE WANTS ME TO HOOK UP WITH SHAYNE. HE'S JUST A HOTTIE & A SWEETHEART. I LOVE JOE. YESTERDAY WE HAD TO BE FIRE FIGHTERS. IT WAS ONE OF THE SCARIEST EXPERIENCES OF MY LIFE. PIGGY IS VERY MOODY. SHE LIKES TO HEAR HER OWN VOICE. CHADWICK THINKS HE IS THE MAN. KEFLA HANGS OUT IN HIS BED A LOT, BUT WHEN THERE'S A MISSION HE'S SO FUNNY. SHAYNE & CHRISTINA ARE AWESOME. NO FIGHTS WITH THEM.

Susie

SUSIE'S DIARY

SUSIE:
Shayne and I would often sleep together in the back of the Winnie. He would never go in for the kill, but I'd know he'd be thinking about getting together. My back would be to him, I'd be sleeping, and I'd feel him going in for the "niceys." He'd start rubbing my back and touching my hips and making a big production of everything. Nothing happened, but it was fun.

SHAYNE: I don't know if you could say that Susie and I had a complicated thing, but, well, I guess it was a thing. At the beginning of the trip, we were flirting a lot and sleeping in the same bed and stuff. But after a few weeks, I had to stop doing that. It just wasn't healthy for me. I'd get all worked up over nothing. Too much energy and no reward.

Susie was fun to flirt with, but we have different morals. She would never have sex before marriage, and I'm not about to give that up. She's a young 18. I know that it really just wouldn't feel right. Still, that doesn't mean I didn't try. I was always kissing her—or at least trying to. I'd get really close, tilt back my head, and wait until she cried, "Ewwwwww!" and ran away.

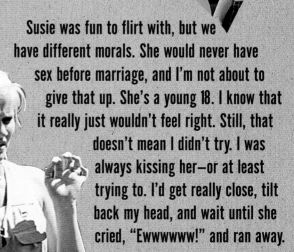

Sydney

Richmond · Berowra
Mulgia · Wallacie
Narellen · Campbelltown
Picton

MISSION

Burn, babies, burn! It's Road Rules Inferno as you fight fire for a day.

FROM PIGGY'S DIARY

Friday 29th February

Definitely the best day for me, which is slightly pathetic as we've all been together now for nearly 2 weeks. Towards the end of the afternoon Brad (one of the fire rescuer instructor) informed us that a storm was brewing. I had been enjoying myself so much, I hadn't noticed that the sky had become begun to cloud. Ah well. What's the reason for the improvement? Early start, always helps – 5:15am today. Plus. I decided to let the terrible twins just play their games – Christina was in a foul mood – she's sick as a dog, and bit my head off – more silent tears, and Susie was a doll, annoyed a little bit. But then I guess I might have been annoying. Anyway, I resolved to be cool and it worked, more or less, the mission – working at the fire station – was brilliant, loved it. We did a beep test, strength test, and had to put out a fire in full apparatus – freaked me out,

and I lost it, felt dumb, but 100°C, and the people were marvelous. I love hanging out w/ men, and they were interested to talk to all of us. Brad was fantastic. I won a jacket! Now I'm just knackered, but good so, done laundry, move on tomorrow, too tired to write any more. Too tired to shower. Too tired!!

CHRISTINA: Fire-fighting was the hardest mission for me. I was feeling so sick. And that day was 7:00 A.M. to 7:00 P.M. straight.

CHADWICK

CHADWICK: <u>Road Rules</u> was a dream come true—a paid vacation to a beautiful land. What more can you ask for?

But did it change my life? Well, my relationship is still a mess. I didn't have anyone to really come home to. And you know what's happened? All these women I haven't talked to in a long time are calling me to get together. I think they just want someone who's on <u>Road Rules</u>. I don't want anything to do with that.

Certainly, I've grown from it. The cameras really change you. It's always been my nature to say whatever's on my mind, but when you've got a camera in your face, you don't want to say anything. So, at first, you're really reserved. Then you get frustrated, and you're like "What the heck?" You reach a comfort level with the cameras and with your environment and with exposing who you are.

SUSIE: Chadwick could be really removed. Sometimes it was like he stood back and watched us on the show, like he was somewhere else.

SHAYNE: Chadwick changed so much during the show. He went from being really uptight to being the life of the party. By the end, all he wanted to do was laugh, smile, and hang out.

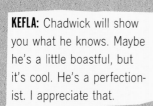

KEFLA: Chadwick will show you what he knows. Maybe he's a little boastful, but it's cool. He's a perfectionist. I appreciate that.

CHRISTINA: Chadwick's done so much in life, you can't help but feel inferior. But he's a really nice guy. Sometimes he'd just drop out. I'd say that he was "entering his web of weirdness." It was like: Where did he go?

PIGGY: All through the show, I was asking Chadwick if he would make out with me. Of course he wouldn't. It was just a joke. But, then, when we were leaving and it was time to say good-bye, he was like: "Don't leave without seeing me first." I got a big hug and kiss. We'd resolved everything.

DATING DOWN UNDER

THE LOST EPISODES OF <u>ROAD RULES VI</u>:

SUSIE: Here's something I'm glad is not going to go on the show. When we were down at Narabeen Beach, we participated in a dating contest. We had no idea what we were going to be doing. Our clue had said: Single Aussies looking for American dates. Uh-oh. I guess we should have known we were about to be tortured.

We were asked to go onstage in front of this audience. We had to sit in rows. There were these two contestants, a guy and a girl, who were asking us questions. It was this whole game-show thing. Each of us had to pretend to be someone else. For instance, Kefla was me. He kept answering questions as if he were me, which is to say that the only response he ever gave was: "I'm a virgin." Ugh.

I guess you could say that we were competing with one another, although I'm not exactly sure any of us wanted to get picked. I mean, they seemed good-looking and everything, but still, it was weird.

The host announced the winners: me and Shayne. When he called me to come and meet my guy, he tried to get me to give him a kiss. "Slip him the tongue!" he screamed. No way.

So we had to go on a date with these people. We were whisked off to a boat, and we went on a little joyride. There was all this good food, huge platters of seafood and crab. It sounds okay, right? Well, it was a complete nightmare. I don't think they'd done a good screening process when they picked our matches, because my date was an ex-convict! He was foul! He kept eating the seafood with his hands and being generally disgusting. I could see that the crew was horrified, because they could barely hold the cameras straight. They were completely laughing.

I turned to Shayne for help, but what a mistake that was. He was too into his girl, who was really pretty. I kept mouthing: "Save me." He just ignored me! But he got his. He was trying to impress his date, thinking maybe he'd get some for once, and guess what happened? He was eating this lobster tail, and he squirted the juice all over her. She was wearing this tube top that she was really into, and she was totally freaking out. He was so embarrassed! I felt bad for him.

All in all, it was a complete <u>Twilight Zone</u> experience.

Lucky me I "win the date." I got to go out with a drunk convict who smokes pot w/ his parents Oh my.

FROM CHRISTINA'S DIARY

Dear God, the humiliation. "Dating Roulette", possibly the equivalent of "Russian Roulette". Place the gun to my head and please do it swiftly. Poor Susie won, and I can't say I'm jealous. Possibly the best luck on the planet. — Oh, to be a loser...

CHADWICK: There was one night when I got drunk. It was really bad. I realized that I'd been removing myself from the group. That upset me, and I think I thought that somehow that would ease tensions with the group. You know, I could relax and kick it with everyone else. What a stupid plan.

Of course it didn't work. No one else wanted to get drunk, and I ended up getting drunk alone. The minute I got into bed, I knew I was going to have to retch. There's one time you don't want to see the cameras. Well, this camerawoman was waiting outside the hostel bedroom door. She followed me as I made a mad dash to the toilet. I was like, "I'm gonna puke. Can't I have some privacy?" Don't you know she stuck the camera underneath the bathroom stall and filmed that way.

It was a really unfortunate experience. It put me off drinking for a while.

SHAYNE'S FAVORITE NAMES FOR BOOZE

1. Wobbly Pops
2. Barley Pops
3. Bowls of Loudmouth Soup
4. Cups of Courage
5. Drunk Dialing (as in: "I was so hammered, I did some drunk dialing, as in "I made some booty calls.'")

MEALS ON WHEELS

I'M YOUR BIGGEST FAN!!!!!

MISSION

Get gourmet as you take it to the highway! With your maître d's, Timmy and Christian from Season Two.

TIMMY: Well, I have to say, I prefer the crazier missions. The more sweat, the better. But I guess dealing with cutlery can pose some sort of a challenge. Cutlery and a moving vehicle; that can get pretty interesting.

I admit I'm biased. I firmly believe that our group, the second season of Road Rules, was hands down, come what may, do what you will, miles and miles of smiles. So it was hard to adapt to a new group. My first instinct was that this group seemed cautious. I was like: "Whoa! What happened? Did they leave the glue back at the woodshop?"

But, you know, each group moves along at its own pace, and they were a really good bunch of people. I liked them all—Christina, Piggy, Kefla, Chadwick, and Shayne and—of course—Susie. Probably no one knows that I knew Susie already? Yep, I did.

I never imagined I'd be the recipient of fan mail, but people are really affected by these shows. There could be a book compiled of all the fan letters we Road Rulers get. Some of the letters are real doozies. One girl called me "smarty pants" 29 times. And one fan sent me money and a ticket, so I could fly to Florida to attend a birthday party. What am I? A clown?

Anyway, Susie sent me my first fan letter. That's right, my very first. It was right after our Road Rules had aired. It was a really touching letter. She actually asked me to go to the prom with her. I felt like Davy Jones. I couldn't go, but we did actually meet. She's from Pittsburgh, just like me, and we hung out at the local radio station, where my season's group was guesting on the show. She was there, and she was sweet. We turned into pen pals.

Imagine my shock when one day I get a letter from her saying: "I just made it through the first round of casting." Whoa. I was like, "What the ????" And then Christian and I are doing a mission with her. Isn't it amazing how this world spins?

SUSIE: A bunch of Road Rulers passed through my town, of course, I had to go meet them! Oh my life, it was awesome!

LETTER FROM SUSIE

DEAR Timmy ♥

I KNOW YOU'RE A BUSY GUY, BUT I JUST WANTED TO WRITE YOU A LITTLE NOTE TO TELL YOU HOW COOL YOU ARE. I FEEL THE PITTSBURGH BOND BECAUSE OF OUR COMMON ROOTS. YOU KICK MAJOR "ROAD RULES" BUTT. I'M GONNA BE PRESIDENT & FOUNDER OF THE "TIMMY FAN CLUB". EVERY MONDAY NIGHT WE SIT AROUND THE TELE & WATCH OUR FAVORITE PITTSBURGHER BATTLE MISSION AFTER MISSION. YOU ROCK. I HOPE ONE DAY TO BE RIDING IN THE WINNIE, LEARNING THE RULES OF THE ROAD. YOU SEEM SO DOWN-TO-EARTH, & COULD YOU BE ANY FUNNIER ?!? YOU'RE A NATURAL ON THE AIR. WANNA GET MARRIED? WE COULD HAVE THE MOST RAD PITTSBURGH WEDDING. — WHAT DO YOU THINK? WELL, LET ME KNOW & GOOD LUCK IN THE FUTURE!

SINCERELY,

Susie ♥

SUSIE: Timmy is just the funniest person ever. I guess you could say I'm guilty as charged. After I wrote Timmy his first fan letter, I became his very own personal stalker! I've been following <u>Road Rules</u> forever.

WHAT'S YOUR PET PEEVE?

SHAYNE: People singing out loud when they've got headphones on. Susie did it all the time! The Spice Girls! Ahhhh!

CHRISTINA: Sweating! It was so hot in Australia, we were always perspiring. We always had rings under our arms, which Shayne called Frisbees. There was this song we made up: "I just want to be Frisbee free!"

SUSIE: Noise in the night, i.e. Chadwick's snoring! Actually, it wasn't really snoring. It was more like long moans. They came from his throat.

CHADWICK: Shayne always has his fingers in his mouth. He's constantly biting his nails.

KEFLA: Rudeness. I hated when the others made fun of Australia right in front of cameramen of Australian descent. Susie and Christina did it the most. I'd have to stop myself from laughing. Because that's plain-out rude.

PIGGY: There's nothing grosser than night sweats, which are what you get when you sleep in the Winnie on a hot night. Chadwick and I would be sleeping together, but we couldn't touch each other—not that we wanted to.

SUSIE'S DIARY

Moreton Island

Deception Bay
gur · Bald Hills
Brisbane
oodridge · Redland Bay
· Beenleigh

MISSION:

Hit the dunes! Toboggan down!
Here's sand in your eyes!

1 YESTERDAY WAS SO RAD. WE WENT TO AN ISLAND CALLED TANGALOOMA. WE HAD TO RIDE DOWN A SAND-DOON ON A PIECE OF WOOD. I WAS FRIGHTENED. AFTER THE 1ST RIDE I WAS HOOKED. I LOVED IT. TALK ABOUT ONCE IN A LIFETIME! LATER THAT DAY WE WENT SNORKLING AND FED DOLPHINS. ALL IN A DAYS WORK I GUESS. TEE-HEE. THE PEOPLE ON THIS TRIP ARE REALLY HORNY. ITS INSANE. PIGGY IS A NICE GIRL, BUT SHE HAS ISSUES & GETS TO FEELING SORRY FOR ~~yourself~~ HERSELF. SHE THINKS SHE'S NOT FUNNY — MEANWHILE SHE IS HYSTERICAL. KEFLA NEVER COMMUNI-CATES UNLESS HE'S MAKING FUN OF ME. IT BLOWS. HE MAKES ME FEEL LIKE I'M SUCH A LOSER. CHADWICK HAS LIKE A MULTIPLE PERSONALITY DISORDER OR SOMETHING. WHEN ITS ONE ON ONE

2 THE TYPICAL "I-DON'T-GIVE-A RATS-BUM" PERSONALITY. SHE WANTS PEOPLE TO THINK IT DOESN'T MATTER TO HER WHETHER SHE'S HERE OR NOT. I KNOW SHE CARES THOUGH. SHE IS DEFINITELY A FUN GIRL & I'M GLAD SHE'S HERE. THE GROUP CAN BE VERY MEAN AT TIMES & SOME TIMES THIS IS THE LAST PLACE I WANT TO BE, BUT TO SEE THIS PLACE & LIVE THIS DREAM IS AB-SOLUTELY AMAZING & I'M THE LUCCIEST GIRL ON THE PLANET. I'VE GOT THE BEST FAMILY, THE BEST BOYFRIEND & I FUTURE SO BRIGHT I HAVE TO WEAR SUNGLAS-SES!!!

3 HE CAN BE REALLY COOL, BUT IF HE FEELS LIKE HE HAS TO PERFORM HE GETS REALLY OBNOXIOUS & BOSSY. HE REALLY TRIES TO PLAY THE PART OF AN OLD SOUL. HE THINKS HE'S THE ONLY ONE w/ EMOTIONAL PROBLEMS CRY ME A RIVER. BUT I DIGRESS. SHAYNE IS COOL WITH ME & IS A SILLY S.O.B., BUT SOMETIMES HE GOES TOO FAR & HURTS MY FEELINGS. HE CAN BE VERY HURTFUL. I THINK HE REALLY THOUGHT HE & I WERE GONNA HOOK-UP OR SOMETHING BE-CAUSE HE CALLS ME A TEASE & AVOIDS TIMES ALONE. POOR GUY, I GUESS ITS MY FAULT. JOE HOLDS MY HEART I'M NOT INTERESTED IN ANYONE ~~ELSE~~ CHRISTINA & I SEEM TO GET ALONG THE BEST. SHE GETS IN THESE MOODS THOUGH WHERE SHE TRIES TO BE

FROM SUSIE'S DIARY

WHO'S THE BEST DRESSED?

SHAYNE: Hands down, Kefla was the best-dressed cast mate. Seriously. He had army days, black-sweatsuit days, jeans days. He was always, always coordinated. He worked at it.

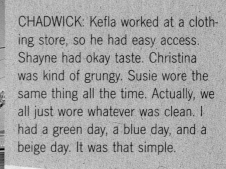

CHADWICK: Kefla worked at a clothing store, so he had easy access. Shayne had okay taste. Christina was kind of grungy. Susie wore the same thing all the time. Actually, we all just wore whatever was clean. I had a green day, a blue day, and a beige day. It was that simple.

MATCHING

KEFLA: I'm really concerned with matching my clothes. I have to match my belt, my shoes, even my underwear. For instance, I will not wear Adidas shoes and Nike socks. I will not wear a CK shirt and Tommy Hilfiger pants. I guess maybe I might wear American Eagle underwear under Tommy Hilfiger jeans, but I would make sure I didn't yawn so you could see them.

My father made me feel like the reason I might end up single is because I didn't match every day. So that's how seriously I take it.

I hated that we didn't have an iron on the trip. I try to keep my groom up.

PIGGY: Oh, big deal, I lost! You know what I say to that: ?!??&#%%$%*?!&#$%*?!&$$#$ %*?!&##$%*! Bollocks!

A BET

CHADWICK: Piggy and I made a bet that she couldn't go a day without swearing. If she lost, she had to give me five bucks. If she won, she got fifty. Pretty good deal, I figured. She needed the money badly. But Piggy failed to make it through even a quarter of the day. At 9 A.M., an hour after we'd gotten up, I went into the Winnebago where Piggy and Susie were hanging around. Susie had just cleaned the Winnie. "How does it look?" she wanted to know. Without a moment's thought, Piggy goes, "F**king brilliant." She looked at me and I laughed. She was toast.

PIGGY

PIGGY: <u>Road Rules</u> can be so hard sometimes; you feel like, "My God! I'm just going to throw myself off a bridge." There's so much self-examination going on. You have all this time on your hands to be with people, and you're almost supposed to not get along with them. And interviews are so draining! If you don't want to talk about something, they make you.

    But, hard as it is, I'm so very glad I did it. You learn tremendous things about yourself and your abilities. Maybe you didn't want to learn them—but you do!

CHADWICK: What I admire most about Piggy is what I hate most: She speaks her mind—even when she doesn't know what she's talking about.

KEFLA: Piggy's a smart girl, there's no denying it.

SUSIE: I love Piggy! Her accent is so fabulous!

CHRISTINA: I compare me and Piggy to Patsy and Edina from the show Absolutely Fabulous. Sometimes it just felt like that. Piggy can be so funny. I'd tell her she was totally "Brit com."

SHAYNE: I wish Piggy wouldn't complain so much. I don't know why she does it. I feel like she tries to get attention when she doesn't need to. I would pay attention to her without her trying.

WEEKLY WORLD NEWS

So you think you're feeling alienated? Investigate some otherworldly sightings and write them up, as you become reporters for the Weekly World News.

WEEKLY WORLD NEWS®

March 8, 1998 $1.25 U.S. $1.39 CANADA/70p U.K.

THE INVASION HAS BEGUN!

ROAD RULERS TO PROBE AUSSIE ALIEN ABDUCTEES!

The outback is crawling with alien abductees and your job is to expose their intergalactic nightmare. Await word from NEWS foreign editor Leskie Pinson — and then prepare to make contact.

CHADWICK BURNS SKY'S LETTER

CHADWICK: I got a letter from Sky in the middle of the trip. We hadn't had any communication since I'd gotten to Australia. But, apparently, she'd gotten the address of the Bunim-Murray offices, gone over there, and dropped off a letter. They sent it to me in Australia. Boy, was I shocked when I received it.

Before I opened it, I didn't know what to expect. My heart was in my throat. I was hoping for reconciliation.

We were taking a walk, all of us, on our way to dinner. I read it on the way. The letter didn't say anything I'd hoped it would say. No "I love you and I miss you" type things. It was more like "I'm sorry it didn't work out." Not what I wanted to hear.

Whenever I hear Sky's voice or see her handwriting, it's totally painful for me, and this was particularly painful. The letter was typed and official-looking, and I felt terrible. Everyone was walking in front of me, and I just let them go ahead. I sat down and cried, sitting on a curb, thinking, God, it's over.

Every time I thought of the letter or glanced at it in my bag, it felt like I was reliving the misery of reading it. I knew I could have just thrown it away, but I needed to do more. I needed to feel renewed. I needed to make a ritual out of it.

So I decided to burn it. I know that sounds dramatic, but I had to. I didn't want to burn it because I hated Sky. I wanted to do it to cleanse myself.

It was morning and everyone was just getting miked up for the day. I took the opportunity to run off on my own without the cameras. I wanted it to be a one-on-one experience between me and God. I took a lighter to the letter and just let it burn to ashes.

I guess it was wrong of me to do it without the cameras watching me. But I didn't feel like there was a way around it. This was something I had to do. It was very personal. It was sacred.

WHO'S MESSIER? THE BOYS OR THE GIRLS?

SHAYNE: The girls! Oh my, their bathroom was always a war zone. Hair in the drain; clothes on the floor. I'm pretty anal, and I thought I was going to be the neatest guy on the trip. But Kefla and Chadwick do everything military style. Folding clothes, packing, everything.

PIGGY: The boys were really clean, almost obsessively so. Doing laundry was a major ordeal. For me, as long as I've got clean knickers, I'm okay.

BOYS NIGHT OUT

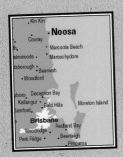

KEFLA: Shayne and I have totally different tastes in women. It's full hips and ass vs. skinny. Shayne likes skinny women, but I have to have humps and bumps, curves and swerves.

SHAYNE: I necked with two girls in one night! Here's how it happened: Chadwick and I met these English girls at a pub. After the pub, we went to the beach to go take a dip, but we couldn't swim there on account of deadly jellyfish. And the beach sucked. There were rocks everywhere, and it was hard to walk.

So we headed back to the pool at one of the girls' place. I'm terrible at making the first move on girls. I just g et all nervous and don't know what to do. So I always put it off until it kind of just happens. I never know what girls are thinking. Does she think I'm ugly? I'm just happy she's hanging out with me.

So, anyway, we're in the pool at her place, and that's where it started. I think it was a joint effort, the first kiss. It was a good time. Everybody likes a little necking.

CHADWICK: I met this woman at the beach, and we kissed. It was my first kiss since Sky. It felt crazy. She was pretty aggressive, and she really caught me off guard. I had an overwhelming sense of guilt. It was as if I still had a girlfriend, although, technically, I guess I didn't. When she told me about her boyfriend of three years, it kind of eased my qualms. Still, it wasn't as joyful as it should have been.

AIRLIE BEACH _____

LOADS OF FUN AT THIS STOP! THE FIVE OTHERS ALL GOT TATTOOS ... I CAN'T BELIEVE IT! ESPECIALLY MY SWEET LITTLE SUSIE... ANYWAY_ SHAYNE AND I ARE BONDING A BIT MORE FROM TIME TO TIME. KEFLA IS STILL TALKING ABOUT GOING HOME EVERYDAY. SUSIE IS STILL LOADS OF FUN, PIGGY AND I GET ALONG MORE THAN WE FIGHT NOW, CHRISTINA. SEEMS FAIR-WEATHERED AT TIMES — BUT STILL A COOL CAT.

WE ALL WENT OUT — STRANGE ENOUGH — SHAYNE AND I MET "THREE WOMEN OF NOOSA" TAM, LOU, CLAIRE. (DO YOU THINK THEIR FOLLOWIN' US?) ANYWAY_ WE ALL WENT DANCING, DRINKING, PLAYIN' ? SINGING... WHAT FUN!!! I THINK CLAIRE LIKED ME — NOT MY TYPE OF WOMAN — I MEAN, SHE WAS FUN AND ALL... BUT TOO YOUNG, TOO 'GREEN' TOO...

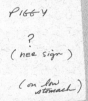

SHAYNE	KEFLA	CHRISTINA	SUSIE	PIGGY
ROAD RULES	ROAD RULES			? (her sign)
(on leg)	(on leg)	(on back)	(on back)	(on low stomach)

ART BY CHADWICK

March 27, 1998

I have a bitchin' tat. We all have them now. Sue got a butterfly, Shayne and Kefla got the Road Rules symbol, Piggy got a scorpio and I have a dragon.

KEFLA'S TATS

KEFLA: Before I got the Road Rules insignia, I already had three tattoos. I have a family tattoo that's represented by Bugs Bunny. Don't ask why. I have one that says "1906," which is the year my fraternity was founded. I had that one done three times over, so it raises up similar to a brand. And I have a picture of King Tut. King Tut is very symbolic to me and my fraternity. We're very into ancient tribes and things of that nature.

SHAYNE'S IDEAL LADY

1. Not worried all the time. Easy-going.

2. Someone who realizes my jokes are just fun and can give it right back.

3. Doesn't wear makeup. I don't like makeup. I even told Susie that I thought she was most attractive with her hair in a bun, no makeup, and jeans on.

4. Athletically inclined. I was almost mad about that. None of the girls in our group played any sports.

CHRISTINA: I was always asking Kefla: "Can I be your main homegirl?" He's so cute!

PIGGY: When we went to Seattle for the Aqua Games, Kefla told me he was going to teach me about being black. I was so thrilled. It's like I don't know anything about my heritage, and he knows so much. We've only begun to explore what we have in common.

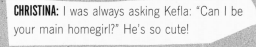

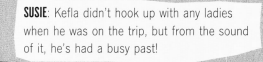

SUSIE: Kefla didn't hook up with any ladies when he was on the trip, but from the sound of it, he's had a busy past!

SHAYNE: Kefla would always say he was going to go off on someone. He'd say he was going to give it to someone for getting on his nerves. He'd say, "It's coming; it's coming." But it never came. I think he's got a fear of confrontation.

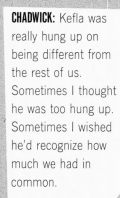

CHADWICK: Kefla was really hung up on being different from the rest of us. Sometimes I thought he was too hung up. Sometimes I wished he'd recognize how much we had in common.

KEFLA

KEFLA: In Foley, Alabama, where I'm from, they don't have MTV. I have it at school, but not at my parents' house. So it was pretty difficult to convince my dad that going on Road Rules was a worthwhile venture. He thought I was just trying to be an entertainer and that I was abandoning my education and the military. My parents are scared of Hollywood. They think it's for other people, not us.

    I tried to explain to my dad that this wasn't an acting gig, but he didn't really understand. He was really upset. He thought I was being hustled. My grandmother was terrified. When she heard Production was getting me a passport, she became convinced that I was involving myself in some massive espionage scandal and that I wouldn't be allowed back in the country.

    I told myself that when I got in front of the cameras, I would represent myself to the fullest. I cared what my friends thought. I cared what my family thought. They're very important to me.

    I don't think Road Rules really changed me. I think it will be a gradual thing. Like maybe in two years, I'll react to a certain situation a certain way. Everyone was so different. I learned from everyone. I was constantly paying attention. I learned from Chadwick, who's accomplished so much. I'm not much for small talk, but Piggy taught me that talking to people—just about this and that—can teach you things. Shayne, even if he wasn't having a good time, he tried. Christina always wanted to know as much as possible. And Susie still has that innocence. I'd like to go back and feel that innocence.

BEING BODY BEAUTIFUL

Move over, Hasselhoff. Take a hike, Yasmeen. The cast of Road Rules VI become lifeguards for a day!

PIGGY: During the lifeguarding mission, they asked us to do these Baywatch-style running-to-the-camera shots. We were wearing bathing suits, mind you. I broke down crying and just couldn't do it. All day, standing in a bikini next to Susie.

CHRISTINA: Body image was a big issue on our trip; it really was. Piggy and I were continually feeling inadequate. Once Piggy and I were looking in the mirror, and she was like, "Could they have cast somebody with bigger thighs?" It was terrible. She's a size 4!!!!

SUSIE: Piggy's pretty proper in most of her eating habits, but give her bacon and she goes to town. She uses all her fingers. It's this elaborate process. First she eats the crunchy part, then she eats the fat strand by strand. Whoa!

I know that Piggy and Christina make a big deal about their bodies, but they're tiny. Christina's got the perfect hourglass figure. She's got that Hungarian blood. But it wasn't like I didn't feel fat often. We had to wear the mikes across our bellies, and Christina and I were always complaining that our stomachs were hanging over the wires. We called them our "goat guts."

CHADWICK: It's true; everybody—including Production—ate fast-food. I was always going off by myself. I'd have to eat alone or I'd fast. That's probably less healthy than eating that stuff, but what can I say?

KEFLA: Piggy says she's fat all the time. She's always complaining. But then she'll wake up in the morning and eat a bacon sandwich, which is basically all fat. It's frustrating. She looks good. And, as I've said before, who wants skinny women?

SHAYNE: Bacon! Bacon! Bacon! If Piggy's metabolism ever changes, she's going to be gargantuan!

PIGGY: Oh, everyone makes such a big deal about bacon, but it's a very English thing to do. If I were living at home, that's what I'd have: bacon and mayo on toast. Those people eat fast-food 24-7. Americans are disgusting!

MISSION

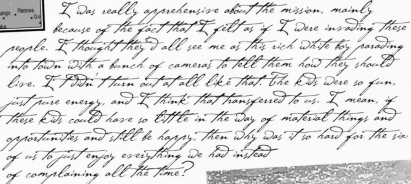

Hit the books, Road Rulers, as you become teachers for a day.

I was really apprehensive about the mission, mainly because of the fact that I felt as if I were invading these people. I thought they'd all see me as this rich white boy parading into town with a bunch of cameras, to tell them how they should live. It didn't turn out at all like that. The kids were so fun, just pure energy, and I think that transferred to us. I mean, if these kids could have so little in the way of material things and opportunities and still be happy, then why was it so hard for the six of us to just enjoy everything we had instead of complaining all the time?

MISSION

First Frocks on the Rocks, now Crocs off the Docks! Be snappy!

SHAYNE: The crocodile mission was my least favorite one. I was a complete wimp about jumping in the pits.

KEFLA: Crocodile meat tastes pretty good, you know. But that was one scary mission, man.

One day in Rockhampton, I was in the Winnie with the rest of the kids going to the caves. This overwhelming urge came over me to be alone, to have some quiet. I faked an illness and had them let me out. Walking back to the hostel, I was hoping no one would be mad at me. They all returned six hours later. Everyone asked me how I was feeling, if I was sick or depressed or tired. Kefla waited until everyone left the room. He said "Hey man, I totally understand. Was it good to be alone?" He told me he escaped all the time.

FROM CHRISTINA'S DIARY

KEFLA: I'm sorry to say that there were times during the trip when I felt I couldn't connect to anybody or anything. To my cast mates, to my surroundings. My cast mates and I, sometimes we just differed — about music, television, everything. And then, Australia was so alienating. There just were not a lot of black people around. That's very foreign to me.

Usually, my sense of humor is what helps me in uncomfortable situations. But I don't always want to play the fool. So I just end up retreating. I go off by myself, or I take a long nap. On this trip, I took a lot of long naps.

There was also a lot of back-talking at this point in the trip—something I wanted to stay far away from. The friends that I hang with back home, we don't flow like that. You talk behind someone's back, eventually you tell them about it. Here, you talk and you don't do jack.

CHADWICK: You don't see this on the show, but Kefla would take a four- or five-hour nap every day. He'd put on his Walkman and enter "Kefla's world" for several hours every day. He never wanted to go out. He was really into his sleep. Then he'd go to bed at around 8:00 P.M. every night. I wish he'd have been able to appreciate the surroundings more. I'd be like, "Man, get up! We're in Australia!" But he wouldn't have any of it.

GIRLFRIENDS

PIGGY: I have a really weird relationship with Christina. Sometimes I
can't figure her out. I think we're really competitive. She's
also really slick. In some ways I adore that about her, and
in other ways I don't. It intimidates me.

FROM CHRISTINA'S DIARY

March 3rd
    Piggy is pouting and sporadically
hysterical because she's convinced ~~Susan~~
(paranoid) that we all hate her.
Especially Susie and myself. She's sure
that Sue and I are much better friends
and have more in common – so we
automatically don't want to be friends
with her. Yes, Sue and I have more in
common, but that doesn't mean we
don't like Pig. It's so frustrating to
deal with Piggy. If Sue and I say
two sentences to each other, Pig belts
out an insecure: "Guys, could you talk
to me. I'm feeling left out."

SUSIE: I have this feeling that Piggy looks worse on the show than she
actually is. I really adore her. I feel like she's my friend. She often
thinks that Christina and I are separating ourselves, but I feel like she
actually instigates that.

    If there's a problem with Christina, it's that she always wants to be
everything to everybody. Depending on the day, you never know whose
best friend she's going to be. She's always up Kefla's bum. Sometimes it
feels like she just has to be the most popular. If the group needs to be
divided up, she's always the one to organize it. And she always puts herself with Kefla and Shayne.

CHRISTINA: Sometimes Piggy and I got
competitive over the stupidest things.
I wore these military pants practically
every single day of the trip. Then, at the
end of the trip, Piggy goes, "You know,
I don't like those! They're not flattering!"
I was like, "You're telling me that now?"

    The thing is I don't get along with
girls that well. We're all like that-Susie,
Piggy, and me. We all find other girls
competitive. I have an easier time with
gay men or just men in general. Susie's
admitted that she's more of a guy's kind
of girl, and I think the same would go for
Piggy. I think it's really important that
girls get along, don't get me wrong.
That's why I regret all the tension we
had with Piggy. But I really tried with her.
Honestly, though, sometimes it's hard to
not feel like she brought it on herself. In
the beginning of the trip, she told me she
was disappointed that there were three
girls on the trip as opposed to two or
four. She said she'd seen a Road Rules
before where there were three girls, and
one of them was completely ostracized.
It was like she wanted it to happen.

CHADWICK: As far as the girls relating to one another goes, I see Piggy as trying not to isolate herself. But then she feels the need to speak her mind, to confront others. She alienates herself without really wanting to.

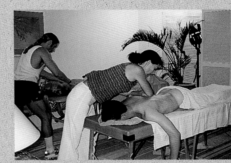

X X X

CHRISTINA: One night when we actually had a motel room, Susie, Piggy, and I rented some porno. No big deal, really. I watch the stuff all the time. And this stuff wasn't really hardcore. Actually, it was barely softcore. But you should have seen Susie! She was freaking out. She had her hands to her mouth the whole time. "Oh, my Lord!" "Oh, my life!" She looked scared. "That looks like it hurts!"

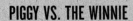

• Rollingstone

Townsville
• Oolbun
Alligator Creek
• Giru

MISSION

Okay, scavengers, go mad! Mad Max, that is. Win and it's spas for everyone!

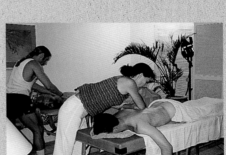

PIGGY VS. THE WINNIE

PIGGY: How devastated I was to crash the Winnie! One of the worst experiences of my life, seriously. It was an all-time low.

WE LOVE U!

TO MY SWEET PICKLE

CHEER UP, CURLY
Keep on truckin'...
With LOVE, Blondie

SUSIE'S CARD TO PIGGY

CHRISTINA: When Piggy crashed the Winnie, the girls took to the streets to make some money. We played our didgeridoo's—although, we're so bad, we should call them didgeridon'ts—and tried to collect cash. We called our band Luscious Beaver, which is the name of a group I'd formed a long time ago with a friend. It's a big joke. We try to be as trashed out and stupid as possible. We made up all these songs. See the inside back cover.

FOOTBALL

CHRIS FROM
SEASON THREE
REPORTS FROM
THE SIDELINES

TOP, (L TO R): OSCAR, RONI,
DAN, CHRIS, BELOU AND EMILY.
BOTTOM (L TO R): SUSIE,
KEFLA, CHRISTINA, SHAYNE,
PIGGY AND CHADWICK

MISSION

Your time has come!
Cast VI, join the ranks
of Road Rules history.

PIGGY AND CHRIS

CHRIS: When they called me to play in the soccer game, I was psyched. Australia! Yeah! But I underestimated how difficult it'd be to get back in front of the cameras. I felt so awkward and uncomfortable! It's funny to think that once upon a time I'd been so at ease.

I didn't know who the other All-Stars would be until I met them at the airport in Los Angeles. Actually, Roni and I flew together from New York, and then we met the others in Los Angeles. I was psyched to see Belou from my season! She got so skinny! And I'd always wanted to meet Oscar and Emily. We got to Australia, checked into the hotel, and then hung out. As a group, we got along tremendously. We were rapping about everything, drinking beers, and going on about our lives. I was digging everyone, especially Roni and Dan from the Northern Trail season.

We met the Season Six cast the next day. My first impression: They're good to look at. The guys were all pretty diesel, and the girls were all pretty.

The game was super fun, if you don't consider the fact that Kefla totally tackled me and I broke my arm. It hurt like hell, but I still couldn't stop laughing at the clinic. That doctor was a quack!

I went from the clinic back to the house, and that's where things took a turn for the weird. We were all staying in this house together, and there was a game set up for us to play in our spare time. It was this strip pool game. You had to answer questions or strip. It wasn't like you had to play—only if you wanted to. Well, Belou didn't want to play, but she had to make a really big deal about it. She went crazy. It was typical old-school Belou. She was screaming about how she didn't want to play, didn't want to take her clothes off, and didn't want to answer the personal questions. I'm used to that stuff, but I think the Season Six cast was a little blown away. She screamed right in Chadwick's face.

But aside from that kind of strangeness, it was a good time. I wouldn't have minded if something had happened with one of the girls, but the opportunity never came up.

OSCAR: I loved their group! There was something to appreciate in each and every one of them.

BELOU

HANDS OFF

PIGGY: The boys from <u>All-Stars</u> were so sweet. Our guys weren't touchy-feely at all. When the other boys showed up, we realized this. I think our guys were paranoid to be shown on camera snuggling up to girls who weren't their mates.

PIGGY AND DAN

DAN: I had so much fun with everybody, especially Susie. Her humor and my humor just really clicked.

EMILY AND SHAYNE

RONI: That group was so nice, so nice! They were awesome!

DAN AND SUSIE

SHAYNE: Emily and I really got along. She was cool to hang out with. The first thing Emily asked me was if our group was hooking up. I explained that the girls all had boyfriends. She told me, "If you and I were on the same trip, we'd totally be getting together."

KEFLA: When we lost the football match, we had to cook for everybody. I did all the cooking. I grilled the steaks; I roasted the vegetables; I made some new potatoes with butter and chives. Oscar fell in love with my cooking. He was like, "Man, move in with me!" You know, I always liked Oscar. I related to the outsider status he had on his trip. So that meant something to me.

After eating, everyone just got up and left. Except Roni. She stayed and helped me clean. She is so well-mannered.

OSCAR, SHAYNE AND KEFLA

CHADWICK: Christina will be a friend to anyone. My mistake was thinking she's always genuine. Sometimes I don't think she means what she says. But, overall, she's a cool cat.

KEFLA: Next to Shayne, I was closest to Christina. She was always willing to put herself out there.

SHAYNE: Christina and I get along really well, but there's never been any sexual tension. I know she's pretty, but I don't really see her that way. She's no girly girl.

PIGGY: Despite our problems, the more I get to know Christina, the more beautiful she becomes to me.

SUSIE: What would I have done without Christina on the trip? She's rad, really rad! And open-minded too! I even got her listening to the Spice Girls!

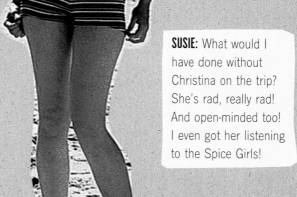

CHRISTINA

CHRISTINA: I'm glad I did Road Rules. I've always known that I suck at human relations, but this was a real slap in the face. You have to be sensitive to the most unexpected things.

Production-wise, everything goes very slowly. The crew works so hard planning everything out. You see the show and think, Wow, they just whipped that out! Think again. You know what's hard? Not looking into the cameras. You don't realize how difficult that can be. And cameras do change the way you behave. At least they did for me. I found myself acting hyperactive. It's like, with cameras around I talk too much.

SUSIE'S GROWING UP

SHAYNE: All the girls got action at the end of the trip. It was a little ironic. The whole trip, they were going on about their boyfriends and being faithful, and getting home. Then, with four more days to go, they start hooking up like mad. It was like, "Oh, I went two and a half months, but I can't go a few more days!"

CHRISTINA: Poor Shayne. I think he was unhappy about Susie and the Australian football star, Shane. The whole time, he felt like she wasn't getting together with him because she had a boyfriend. And then she goes and messes around with someone she barely knows. It hurt him.

SHANE AND SUESIE

Driving too much lately pushes me over the edge of insane boredom. I really have grown to love everyone and we've managed to overlook our unchangeable differences. Piggy seems happier than ever, throwing little or no tantrums. I think she's connected more with the boys. The feeling of acceptance is all she needs to be happy. Susie is swinging out loads more lately; stealing bowling shoes, taking a sip of my long island iced tea, getting a tattoo; and changing her clothes in front of us. She's not as Prudish as in the beginning. Thank God!

FROM CHRISTINA'S DIARY

SUSIE: During the football mission, I flirted with Dan. I love Dan. We had a whole dance party with Michael Jackson and Madonna. And then, sleeping in the same bed with him, I could tell why they called him "the whisper twin." He's just a chatty Patty in the sack.

But the real love of my Road Rules trip was Shane, the Australian football star. It was a big deal for me to betray my boyfriend at home for someone else, but I had to do it. Piggy's the one who convinced me to call him. She was like, "Come on, he's got a Beemer and he's 23."

That first night we hung out was great, but he was super-duper nervous about the cameras. I guess because he's famous and everything. He kept passing me these secret notes:

I feel uncomfortable.   *I want to be alone.*   *I wish these cameras would piss off.*

We finally stole upstairs, where we made out. He was so paranoid the whole time. It was like the forbidden fruit, running away from the cameras.

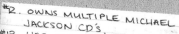

From Susie's diary:

AND NOW- THE MOMENT YOU'VE ALL BEEN WAITING FOR:

WHAT HAPPENED WITH ♡♡♡ SHANE CRAWFORD?

I MUST ADMIT, THIS IS ONE OF MY PROUDEST ACCOMPLISHMENTS. HELLO? COULD HE BE ANY MORE PERFECT. OH MY LIFE. LIST OF THINGS SHANE'S GOT GOING FOR HIMSELF:

#1. H-O-T
#2. SEEMINGLY NOT A JERK.
#3. HELLO, ABS!
#4. OWNS HOME
#5. PROFESSIONAL ATHLETE.
#6. NO VISIBLE SCARS
#7. FULL HEAD OF HAIR
#8. POLITE
#9. LOADED
#10. SINGLE
#11. PLAYS DRUMS (MUSIC IS CRUCIAL)

#12. OWNS MULTIPLE MICHAEL JACKSON CD'S.
#13. HAS HIS OWN TV SHOW
#14. NOT A PIG (OPENLY, AT LEAST)
#15. DECORATED HIS OWN HOME
#16. HAS RED BMW
#17. GOT HIS MUM A TRIP TO HONG KONG - JUST 'CAUSE!
#18 DIDN'T MENTION ONCE THAT I WAS 18
#19 KNOWS HOW TO SURF
#20 KNOWS THE WORDS TO "CAN'T GET ENOUGH OF YOUR LOVE BABY" POPULARIZED BY BARRY WHITE
#21 NEVER ONCE TRASH TALKED HIS EX-GIRLFRIEND.
#22 WAKES UP EVERY MORNING TO RUN AT 5:00 A.M.
#23 BOUGHT EVERYONE DRINKS, BUT DIDN'T DRINK HIMSELF
#24 GOOD KISSER ☺

DON'T THINK THAT JUST BE-CAUSE I WAS DISTRACTED (MILD UNDERSTATEMENT) BY SHANE THAT DIDN'T TAKE NOTE OF MY SWEET LAMB, DAN FROM SEASON 1. HE IS A CUTEY. I'VE GOT SUCH A CRUSH ON HIM. HE'S ONE OF THOSE PEOPLE WHO MAKES EACH GIRL FEEL VERY SPECIAL. HE LOOKS IN YOUR EYES + SPEAKS W/ SUCH A GENTLE DEMEANOR. IT'S NO WONDER GIRLS FALL FOR HIS CHARMS. I HOPE I KEEP IN TOUCH WITH HIM.

PIGGY: Susie's religion tells her she can't, but her body tells her, "C'mon, girl! Let's go!" Of course, she was going to get together with Shane Crawford. I told her she'd regret it if she didn't. I myself had a footie man, but it wasn't as big a deal. But, it was nice to get a little.

MISSION

The party's over! Sky Dive down to your handsome rewards.

CHRISTINA: The minute I touched the ground, it was like, "We did it! We did it!" Suddenly, I felt this tremendous sense of accomplishment.

KEFLA: Skydiving, I realized that I'd gotten everything I'd prayed for. I'd prayed to be on this show; I'd prayed to get a motorcycle; I'd prayed I'd make it through all the missions. If I didn't feel blessed, I'd be a fool.

CHADWICK: I was so jazzed to have my handsome reward. It was a long time coming, and I felt a big sense of pride and relief.

SHAYNE: Skydiving, I realized I was scared to go home. I've changed so much. I have talked and opened up so much. I'm scared I won't know how to act around my friends, who've all stayed home and remained the same.

SUSIE: Flying in the air, I kept thinking that before this trip I'd never been away from home. And now look at me.

PIGGY: I hit the earth and remembered how it had all begun—with diving off those cliffs and feeling so petrified. It was great to know I'd done it all.

145

Christina & Oscar

CHRISTINA: When I first met Oscar at the football match, I thought he was crass and rude. He kept pulling my hair. I was like, "Oh, my God, can you grow up at all?" But then one night we got into this major conversation. Actually, Belou and Dan were there, too. It was this conversation about how much of yourself you give to <u>Road Rules</u>. Well, they all got pretty dramatic about

FROM CHRISTINA'S DIARY

I think Oscar is so blunt with new people to shock them and see if they are phonies. I like that. If you give him a real response to his obnoxiousness, he steps down and becomes a playful person. Belou was interested in him from the day they landed in Australia. (I guess about a day or two before we met them.)

the whole thing. I mean, tears started flowing. Belou and Oscar both. Actually, all of us. I was like, "Whoa, there's another side to Oscar." Seeing him cry, just changed my entire opinion.

Surprise, surprise, there weren't enough beds at the house where we were staying. So Oscar and I ended up sharing a bed, but he didn't try anything. He was so decent. I guess I kind of got off on it, because all of a sudden, I was feeling like I liked him. Suddenly, I just wanted to be all "Hey, baby."

The minute we got back to L.A. after our final reward, I got together with Oscar. I call him my Puerto Rican firecracker. He's adorable. We would totally have gone crazy if we'd been on the same trip.

She would tell me about how much Oscar reminded her of the guy she was married to. If Oscar would do so much as look at me, Belou would give us both the evil eye. The worst of it came the night Oscar and I ~~sl~~ slept in the same bed together in the mansion. Granted, nothing happened, but Belou was furious with us both. She pulled me aside and asked me if I had feelings for him. If I did, she would leave us both alone. Of course, I did not (at the time). Oscar was then and still is someone I adore, but am not in love with. Belou was so upset that Oscar didn't like her back.

OSCAR FINDS LOVE

SUSIE: Christina and Oscar, they're just made for each other.

OSCAR: When I first saw Christina on the playing field, I thought she was incredibly sexy. I hadn't even talked to her. I think I might have fallen in love with her hair. That beautiful blonde hair. She has all these light hairs on the back of her neck. They were so sexy to me. All the other guys were "Susie, Susie, Susie," but not me. I was like, "I think I like that other one."

She seemed kind of snobby at first, but I'm usually attracted to girls like that. Either I want to get past all their barriers, or I want to make their lives hell for being such snots. I guess we crossed some barriers when we started burping together.

That first night in the mansion was fun, but our romance didn't really get going until the wrap party for the show. See, after the football game, Roni and I stayed in Australia for a few days. We backpacked around Sydney, stayed in a youth hostel, and met the gang for their final party. Knowing I was going to see Christina again, I wanted to get her something special, a little gift. Roni helped me pick out a pair of earrings.

She looked so pretty at the wrap party, so pretty. The second I saw her, I pulled her aside. "I don't want to intimidate you with what I'm about to do," I warned her. "But I just want to thank you for being such a great human being." Then I pulled out the earrings. They were in this nice box, and when she opened it, wow, she was just in total shock.

We ate dinner together, and then we took a walk through Sydney's red-light district. It was the nastiest, skankiest neighborhood, but we had a good time looking at everything. Then we went back to the hotel room and had fun. The next morning, we said good-bye.

I saw her in Los Angeles one more time. Honestly, I don't usually get so excited about seeing girls. She's different, though. She's just something else. I don't know when I'll see her again, but I know I will. I have to.

Kefla & Roni

KEFLA: I was star-struck when I saw Roni first walking across the football field. I saw those locks, and I knew it was her. I was so happy. I was hoping she'd be on the other team. I wanted to meet her and talk to her so much, but I didn't want to act like a giddy 13-year-old. I wanted to get her autograph. That's not exactly a swift move.

Ever since I saw her on Road Rules, I'd been thinking about her. I even had a dream about her. In the dream, I was in New York City. Roni and I were going out to dinner. We had a great time, and afterward, we ended up hooking up. It was so beautiful and so real. So, imagine, I had this vivid dream, and then there she is in person. Wham! The truth is, she's more beautiful in person than I could have ever imagined. She's gorgeous, actually—inside and outside. Much to

everyone's dismay, we didn't end up hooking up after the football game. It just wasn't right. All the cameras, all this pressure. I really wanted to be a gentleman.

I thought the football game would be the last time I saw her. But then there she was at the wrap party. We'd gotten our final reward. There were no more cameras. The show was over. I was in a good mood, happy to be going home and happy to finally be partying with the crew. I was really in my element. I was wearing a fitted shirt and jeans, and I had my cowrie-shell necklace on. I was feeling fine.

Cowrie shells are really important to African Americans. It used to be that cowrie shells were used to purchase slaves. They're a symbol of everything we've been through. Well, wouldn't you know, there's Roni across the room, all beautiful and glowing. I had no idea she was still in Australia. Before I can make it across the room to talk to her, I notice that she's wearing a cowrie shell in her locks. I was so pleased.

I was so happy to see her, I just gave her a hug. We went to dinner and took a picture together. I'll cherish that picture forever. We're both smiling. She's someone I'd want to have as a friend forever.

After dinner, a bunch of us went to a hip-hop club. Piggy was like, "Wow, I'm finally seeing you dance!" I guess I just seemed like a different person—relaxed and happy. So Roni and I were dancing. She's a really good dancer, but whatever she could do, I could do. We were good together. If you're making that deep eye contact with someone, you know you've really connected. They were playing reggae, and we were just all over the floor. I think she was surprised I could move at all. After all, I'm just a little country boy.

We walked back to the hotel holding hands. I hugged her good-bye and thanked her for an amazing evening. I thought that was going to be it, but she just wouldn't let go of me. She held me for longer than I expected. Here I was trying to be this gentleman, trying to be everything girls say guys can't be. I didn't want to go overboard. But I had to kiss her. At first it was just a little kiss, but then it got longer and more passionate. Oh my, it was amazing. We stopped after a while. I gave her a peck on the cheek. "Have a safe trip home," I told her.

Walking back to the hotel, I was smiling ear to ear. I just was hitting myself. "Do you know what you just did? You kissed a beautiful girl!"

I wouldn't change anything about Roni. Except maybe her ZIP code. Actually, I take that back. I'd change my ZIP code. That way, she'd stay perfect.

RONI: That night, Kefla was so cute. The wrap-party night, oh my goodness. He just grows on you so fast.

I wish he'd had more fun on his trip, but I understand exactly what he was going through. It's hard to open up when you feel so alienated. God, we would have had so much fun if we'd been on the same Road Rules.

Australia, that was my chance to come back and try again, to really be myself. I didn't want to be as closed off as I'd been on my trip. I wanted to be what I'm usually like: happy, not uptight. It was funny to have the cameras on me, looking for romance. That was not a role I played on my trip. I was more like a side player. So it was a little overwhelming to have all this pressure on me. All the girls were like, "Do you like Kefla? You know he likes you?" I just couldn't handle it.

I'm so glad we managed to have a night to ourselves. I have a copy of the picture that was taken of us. I carry it around with me everywhere. He's just a really good kisser. I mean, really good. Sometimes, it just works.

KEFLA: I was closest to Shayne. Even if he didn't match his clothes!

PIGGY: Shayne's got a good attitude. I found it infectious sometimes.

CHRISTINA: Shayne and I were like brother and sister during the trip.

CHADWICK: Shayne made me realize that whatever happens, you can always laugh about it. We totally bonded during the last few weeks of the trip.

SUSIE: Shayne, Shayne. King of niceys! We'll be buds for good.

SHAYNE

SHAYNE: We don't have MTV in Canada, but there are three or four pubs that have satellites. Some friends are planning to get together and have drinks while watching the show. I may go to those pub nights, but I've decided that I'm going to watch the shows alone first. The producers send you a tape early, and I feel like that will be the best way to do it: watch the show alone and prepare myself for the crap my friends are going to give me. My friends are a sarcastic group. We don't really go for all the feelings talk. When they see me in my interviews, opening up and talking about feelings, they're going to rip into me.

Being a Canadian, it's hard for me to understand that the show is a big deal. Susie says we're going to have fans. It's crazy, but when we were in the airport in Melbourne, this group of American teenagers chased us, asking for autographs. And we hadn't even been on television yet!

WHERE ARE THEY NOW?

YOU'VE BEEN INDUCTED INTO THE HALL OF ROAD RULES FAME!

PIGGY: The night we got back from Australia, we had a night in Los Angeles before getting our flights home. Tara called us at the airport hotel and asked us if we wanted to hang out with a bunch of Road Rulers from the past. Since Christina was going to be seeing Oscar anyway, it made sense. So we all went out. It was Vince and Oscar from the Islands season, Devin from Season Two, Tara, and Syrus from The Real World. We drank and hung around and went to Jerry's Deli for a late-night snack. It was fun. Susie was star-struck, of course; she knows every-thing about every last cast member.

SUSIE: Hanging out with all those ex-Road Rulers was bizarre. It's this whole big family. Everyone looks out for one another. It's rad. It's totally rad.

PIGGY

It's really hard to know what to do after Road Rules. I certainly don't want a desk job. I participated in a pilot for TV, and we'll see what happens with that. I'm still living in my little but beautiful apartment in Marin County. I think I'll stay here. I'm not seeing anyone now. Being single is fun! I've been mak-ing a lot of new friends-including Jason from Real World-Boston. He and Timber moved nearby!

CHADWICK

CHADWICK: Coming back from Road Rules was kind of tough. It was sort of like I hit the ground running. Trying to get back into the swing of things can be weird. Spending months when your only responsibility is participating in missions and getting along with people—that can be kind of surreal. I'm back to my busy lifestyle. I got accepted at Harvard for graduate school, but I'm not sure whether I'm going to go. I'm working at the gym full-time training. My relation-ship with Sky is still up in the air. I'm still in love with her.

JEREMY (CHRISTINA'S BOYFRIEND): Christina claims to not be going through withdrawal, but I know she is. It's rough to go back to normal life with no cameras and no missions!

SUSIE

SUSIE: After <u>Road Rules</u>, I got a job on a movie production in Pittsburgh. I watched the crew members on the road, and it looked really cool to me to be on the other side of the cameras. Next fall, I'm enrolling in the University of Pittsburgh. That's right: No more community college for me. I'm still living at home, but Piggy and Christina want me to move out to San Francisco to be with them. It's tempting! As for boys, I'm not seeing anyone seriously. When I got home, I gave Shane Crawford a call. He never called back. I tried again. Nothing. I didn't realize he was such a player! I'm bitter!

SHAYNE

SHAYNE: I'm finishing up my final semester at the University of Alberta. I'm getting a Bachelor of Commerce degree. It'll be a never-ending job search, but I'll manage. I'm bartending now. It'd be great to move to the States. I think <u>Road Rules</u> means a lot more on your résumé when you get out of Canada.

KEFLA

KEFLA: I'm back at Alabama State as a senior. I'm the Hornet again. My little brother and sister are coming up to live with me. They just got out of high school, and I told my family that if anyone wanted to go to school, they'd always have a place to stay with me. As far as plans beyond school go, a couple of people in Production told me I should seriously think about trying to do stuff in front of the camera. I don't know about that. I do know I need to apply for grad school soon, and I want to move somewhere else. I might have to go up North—even though I can't stand the cold weather.

CHRISTINA

CHRISTINA: I'm back in San Francisco, living with my friends and finishing up school. I think to some degree we all want <u>Road Rules</u> to be a springboard to something bigger and better. I don't know. I think I better stick with life off camera for a while, hang out with people I love, and study.

REUNITED AND IT FEELS SO GOOD!!!!!

ROAD RULES VS. REAL WORLD

Seattle

KEFLA: I started missing the trip once I was home, and I was really happy to know I was going to have another chance to see my cast mates. Plus, I was eager to meet the Real Worlders. It felt like we were going to meet our long-lost distant cousins, and I just wanted to check them out.

I loved going to Seattle. It wasn't like going to Australia, where I had nothing to grasp on to. Seattle was great. It was different, but familiar to me, and I was comfortable. Actually, I was happy, really happy. On my first night there, I had an unforgettable experience. I've been playing baseball my whole life, but Alabama doesn't have a professional team. Well, the second I was in Seattle, I knew I had to go to a Mariners game. When I first saw the field, it took my breath away. I even saw Ken Griffey Jr. play center field. To actually see the pop flies go by your head, my God.

That night, everyone else went out drinking. I had something of a revelation. In Australia, that's how it had been: Everyone went off drinking and I stayed on my own. I had blamed that on the fact that we were in Australia and I was feeling out of place. But here I was doing it again. It made me think:

Maybe I'm just different. It was really kind of a relief.

The morning of the competition, I was psyched. We'd already been snooping around. We were asking people in the hotel about the Real Worlders. Had they seen them around town? What were they like? They said they had seen them and that they were stuck-up. They warned us that the guys were big. Then they told us the girls were little. I had it in me that we were going to be kicking some brats' asses.

I expected to be intimidated by the guys, but I wasn't—not at all. Maybe they had two inches over me, but size-wise and strength-wise, I was not worrying. Yeah, they were in the military, but, hey, I went through Air Force basic training, I'm in the Reserve, there's no difference. I was probably thicker than two of them. I was thinking, Hey, I'm cool. Overall, those Real Worlders were a good-looking cast. They were all cool. They had some very attractive girls. Janet was really pretty. Lindsay had a glowing personality, and Rebecca was cool. But, of course, straight up, none can compare to Roni.

Our group was getting along really well. I probably talked to Susie this time more than anybody else. We were just clicking. In many ways, Susie and I have a lot in common.

Neither of us drink or smoke or feel the need to go out all the time. I don't know why it took us so long to realize that. This time around, we were talking and laughing. She's grown up a whole lot. I applaud it. But I feel for her. It's a tough thing to do to go through a big change and then have to go back and live with your parents. That's a tough thing to do. I mean, to some degree we all changed, but she gained the knowledge that she can make it on her own. She's almost like two different people. It's so nice. She's got a sense of independence about her.

I'm sorry that we didn't come through on the competition. I like to look at it as if I lost it for us. We had to dive through these rings, and I missed the ring. I want to take that responsibility. From the second we got there, the girls were like, "Kefla, we're counting on you." They always wanted me to be team captain. We were all sad, but I probably took it harder than anyone else. I hate losing. Once you taste victory, defeat will never go down the same. I tried to hint around to the executive producers that if there's any kind of All-Stars thing, they should let me be in it. I want to redeem myself.

That night, we had to do a skit competition. We had to make up a song about the other cast. It had to be creative and original. <u>The Real World</u> went first. They were dissing our Winnebago real bad. They were going: "<u>Road Rules</u> is a messed up gig. You're the sequel to a real show." They were just putting us down.

We were messing around the whole time. We kept procrastinating. Susie volunteered me to be captain. I told them to just make up some music, and I'd do a solo rap, making up the

PIGGY: It was so good to be back together for the Aqua Games. When Christina and I saw Susie, it was so exciting. We were jumping up and down.

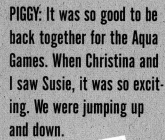

We're six spoiled brats
And we're living for free
If you ask me where I live, and I'll tell you
Pier 70

Stephen, my man, the size of your feet is unbelievable
If you stood upon your tiptoes, you could look over the
Space Needle

We're six conceited brats
And we're living for free
When I get back home, I'm going to say to my friends
Hey, you know, I'm on
MTV

KEFLA'S NOTES

THE PREMIERE PARTY

SHAYNE: We saw one another and <u>The Real World</u> cast one more time. There was a premiere party in L.A., and we all got to go. In Seattle, I'd been chatting up Lindsay. She's short and cute. What can I say? That's right up my alley. So I was psyched to see her again.

The party was a complete blast. Nathan and I were doing shots of tequila, so I have foggy memories of the night. Let's just say at 2:00 A.M., I showed up in Lindsay and Janet's hotel room wearing nothing but my underwear.

LINDSAY: Shayne's a good-looking guy. It was fun to hang out with him. I made fun of his accent the whole time. There were some sparks between us, definitely. But what could we do? There wasn't a whole lot of time when we were in Seattle.

In L.A., he actually ended up hanging out with Janet more than with me. When he showed up in our room in CK briefs, he jumped into her bed, not mine. But I don't think anything happened.

ROAD RULES is about the adventures of six young people, women and men, who will travel to unknown destinations and accomplish a series of adventures. We're not interested in hiring six actors—we want real people from varying ethnic and socio-economic backgrounds—we want the conventional and the not-so-conventional. This is not an experience for a wallflower. If selected, you will be one of these six people.

SO YOU WANT TO BE ON ROAD RULES?

We're looking for interesting people who are not afraid to express their opinions, people who want to share their lives...all in front of the cameras. You'll be living in a fishbowl, with cameras rolling almost every hour of every day, wearing a wireless microphone and having two or three camera people following you around—in the vehicle, on the street, on dates and sometimes when you're desperate just to be left alone. Consider this very carefully because we'll require you to sign a contract to commit for the full shooting period of approximately ten weeks.

This is a tough, emotionally exhausting experience. Think about whether you have the strength to endure it. If you are still interested, send in an application right away!

ROAD RULES APPLICATION INSTRUCTIONS

1 Fill out the enclosed application legibly. **2** Attach a recent photo of yourself, a copy of your passport or birth certificate, and a copy of your driver's license. **3** Make a ten-minute videotape of yourself talking about whatever you think makes you a good candidate for Road Rules. Remember, we want to see if you are a person who is open and willing to express what is important to you. Sometimes the best videos are very simple. Don't overthink it, and try to be honest and sincere. (also, make sure there's enough light on your face and that you are close enough to the mike to be heard.) **4** Send the application package (make sure you have the correct postage!) to: Road Rules - Casting Dept., 6007 Sepulveda Blvd., Van Nuys, CA 91411. Please note that anything you send us becomes the property of Bunim/Murray Productions, so don't send anything that you'll need to get back. **5** We will contact you further from this point. Please be patient.

ROAD RULES APPLICATION FORM

NAME: _____

ADDRESS: _____

PHONE: _____

Age: _____ Birthdate: (You must be 18-24 years old to be on Road Rules) _____

Parents' Names, Address, Phone: _____
_____
_____
_____

Brothers and sisters (names and ages): _____
_____

Are you or have you ever been a member of SAG/AFTRA? (circle one) Y or N

Have you ever acted or performed OUTSIDE of school? (circle one) Y or N _____
_____

Name of high school (with years completed): _____
_____

Name of college (with years completed and majors): _____
_____
_____

Other education: _____
_____
_____

Are you currently in school? (circle one) Y or N

Do you work? If so, describe your job. _____
_____
_____
_____

What will you miss the most about leaving your friends and family for 10 weeks? _____
_____
_____
_____

What will you miss the least? _____
_____
_____

How would you describe your best traits? _____
_____
_____
_____

How would you describe your worst traits? _____
_____
_____
_____

Have you ever treated someone you cared about in a way that makes you proud?
Tell us about it. _____
_____
_____
_____

Have you ever treated someone you cared about in a way that you regret?
Tell us about it. _____
_____
_____
_____

How long does it take you to get ready in the morning? Do you consider yourself high maintenance or low maintenance? Why? _____
_____
_____
_____

If you could only pack one backpack for the trip, what would be in it? _____
_____
_____
_____
_____

Describe your most embarrassing moment. _____
_____
_____

Do you have a boyfriend or girlfriend? (circle one) Y or N

How did you meet? How long have you been together? What drives you crazy about the other person? What is the best thing about the other person? _____
_____
_____
_____
_____
_____

How would your boyfriend/girlfriend feel about you leaving for 10 weeks?
Would you be faithful? _____
_____
_____

Other than your boyfriend or girlfriend, who is the most important person in your life right now? Describe him/her and why he/she is important. _____
_____
_____
_____

How important is sex to you? Do you have it only when you're in a relationship or do you seek it out at other times? What's the most exciting/interesting place you've ever had sex?
_____
_____
_____
_____

Is there any issue, political or social, that you're passionate about? Have you ever done anything about it? _____
_____
_____
_____

What is the most important issue or problem facing you today? _____
_____
_____

Are you physically fit? _____
_____

Do you work out? If so, how often and what types of activities do you like to do? If not, how do you stay in shape? _____
_____
_____

Describe a major event or issue that has affected your life: _____
_____
_____

What habits do you have that we should know about? _____
_____
_____
_____

What habits do other people have that you simply cannot tolerate? _____
_____
_____
_____

Describe how conflicts were handled at home as you were growing up
(Who won? Who lost? Was yelling and/or hitting involved?). _____
_____
_____
_____

What are your thoughts on abortion? _____

On sexual orientations different from your own? _____

On welfare? _____

Where were you born? Where did you grow up? _____
_____

Have you traveled around the United States?
Describe some experiences you enjoyed and some you didn't. _____
_____
_____

Tell us about some places in the United States you have always wished you could visit and why. _____
_____
_____
_____

What do you do on the weekend for fun? _____
_____
_____

If you had Aladdin's lamp and three wishes, what would they be? _____
_____
_____

Name three living people you would like to meet and why. _____
_____
_____

Where do you see yourself in five years (personally and professionally)? _____
_____

Ten years? _____
_____
_____

What was the last unusual, exciting or spontaneous outing you instigated for you and your friends? _____
_____
_____

Do you smoke cigarettes? (circle one) Y or N
Do you drink alcohol? How old were you when you had your first drink? How much do you drink now?
How often? _____
_____
_____
_____

Do you use recreational drugs? What drugs have you used? How often? _____
_____
_____
_____

Are you on any prescription medication? If so, what and for how long have you been taking it? _____
_____
_____

Have you ever been arrested? If so, what was the charge and were you convicted? _____
_____
_____

Have you had any traffic tickets? If so, how many? _____
Has your license ever been suspended? If so, why? _____
_____
_____

Do you believe in God? Are you religious? Do you practice religion? _____
_____
_____

Who are your heroes and why? _____
_____
_____

When you do something ridiculous, how much does it bother you to have other people notice it
and laugh at you? _____
_____
_____

How do you rate on the following?
(Rate yourself on a 1 to 10 scale, 1 being unskilled, and 10 very skilled)

RATING	ACTIVITY	COMMENTS
_____	Riding a bicycle	_____
_____	Riding a motorcycle	_____
_____	Skiing	_____
_____	Running a mile	_____
_____	Snowboarding	_____
_____	Rock climbing	_____
_____	Surfing	_____
_____	Speaking a foreign language	_____
_____	Fixing a car	_____
_____	Fixing a motor	_____
_____	Fixing a flat tire	_____
_____	Cooking	_____
_____	Sewing	_____
_____	Tying nautical knots	_____
_____	Sailing a boat	_____
_____	Swimming	_____
_____	Skydiving	_____
_____	Water-skiing	_____
_____	Scuba diving	_____
_____	Using a computer	_____
_____	Driving a bus	_____
_____	In-line skating	_____
_____	Bungee jumping	_____
_____	Setting up a tent	_____
_____	Reading a map	_____

List 4 people who have known you for a long time and will tell us what a
great person you are (excluding relatives).
Name / Address / Phone / How Do They Know You?

1. _____
_____
_____

2. _____
_____
_____

3. _____
_____
_____

4. _____
_____
_____

I acknowledge that everything stated in this application is true. I understand that any falsely submitted answers can and will be grounds for removal from the application process and from subsequent participation in the final series. I further acknowledge and accept that this application form and the videotape I submit to MTV will become property of MTV and will not be returned. By signing below, I grant rights for MTV-Bunim/Murray Productions (BMP) to use any biographical information contained in this application, my home video, or taped interview, and to record, use, and publicize my home videotape or taped interview, voice, actions, likeness, and appearance in any manner in connection with Road Rules.

Signature _____

Date _____